Contents

A STATEMENT FOR THE Y-12 FACILITY

Come let us go up
to the mountain of God
to the house where God lives.
That God may teach us God's ways
That we may walk in God's paths. . . .

For God will bring justice among the nations and bring
peace between many peoples. They will hammer their
swords into plowshares
and their spears into pruning hooks. Nations will not
lift swords against nations. No longer will they learn
to make war.
Come, let us walk in the light of God. Isaiah 2

Brothers and sisters, powers that be, we come to you
today as friends, in love. We, like many of you, are people
of faith, inspired by many who have gone before us, people
like the prophets, Isaiah and Micah, Jesus as well as Gandhi,
and the countless who call us "to beat swords into plowshares." May we now transform weapons into real, life-
giving alternatives, to build true peace.

We come to the Y-12 facility because our very humanity
rejects the designs of nuclearism, empire and war. Our faith
in love and nonviolence encourages us to believe that our
activity here is necessary; that we come to invite transformation, undo the past and present work of Y-12; disarm and
end any further efforts to increase the Y-12 capacity for an

economy and social structure based upon war-making and empire-building.

A loving and compassionate Creator invites us to take the urgent and decisive steps to transform the US empire, and this facility, into life-giving alternatives which resolve real problems of poverty and environmental degradation for all.

We begin together by preparing our minds and hearts for this transformation. And so we bring gifts to symbolize this transformation, instruments that serve life, peace and harmony, truth and healing to this nuclear weapons plant and everywhere.

We bring our life-symbols:

-blood, for healing and pouring out our lives in service and love. Our very humanity depends on lives given, not taken. But blood also reminds us of the horrific spilling of blood by nuclear weapons.

-our hammers, to begin the transforming work of deconstructing war machines, creating new jobs which address real problems, eliminate poverty, heal and foster the fullness of life for all.

We bring our truth-symbols:

-candles, for light transforms fear and secrecy into authentic security.

-flowers, the White Rose of forgiveness, acceptance of friendship and genuine reconciliation.

-the crime tape and an Indictment, which point out truth and end lies which have blinded and dulled the very conscience of nations, and serve the interests of justice for healing global relationships.

-a Bible, to remind ourselves to become sources of wisdom and to inspire our acts of conscience as we carry on.

Lastly we bring food, symbolized by this bread, strengthening us as we build this new world where people do not feel compelled to build nuclear weapons in order to feed their families. So may we break and share this bread together in joy and genuine friendship as we work together, empowered by our Creating God

TO TRANSFORM NOW!

Michael Walli   Greg Boertje-Obed   Megan Rice shcj

Transform Now Plowshares

Editorial Note

Sr. Megan Rice, SHCJ, died shortly before this book's publication. However, the author consulted her on all of it, and she was pleased with the cover. She is shown tucked safely between Michael and Greg, whom she considered her protectors, just as when they entered the free-fire "kill zone" of a nuclear warhead facility.

A few days before Sr. Megan died, Sr. Clare Pratt, RSCJ, and the author visited her at the Holy Child Center in Rosemont, Pennsylvania. She beamed contentedly, but was uncharacteristically frail and quiet. Both sisters received Holy Communion from a volunteer minister while the author was out getting their lunch. They enjoyed a time of shared silence, and then Sr. Clare sang "Let Us Break Bread Together" to Sr. Megan. After the food arrived, Sr. Megan took two crackers from the lunch, held them up, and then handed them to her guests with a questioning smile. An attempt to share Eucharist, perhaps? Before they left, one of them placed sunflower blossoms in individual cups all over her room. They didn't know it would be their last visit. She slipped away later that week surrounded by SHCJ sisters and family members, including her namesakes Megan #2 and Megan #3. Those sunflowers, a universal symbol of nuclear disarmament, were all around her.

The book now remains just as it was when she was with us. The author didn't wish to revise into the past tense, and it is still dedicated to Sr. Ardeth Platte, OP, as Megan surely would have insisted.

So in union with the communion of saints, we hope you will join us in saying (and praying), with abundant gratitude for her life's work, Sr. Megan Rice, SHCJ, *¡Presente!*

Preface

Liturgical Press initially imagined this as a book about one anti-nuclear activist, Sr. Megan Rice, written by a different author. I came to the project in early 2017, when Rice and I were neighbors in Washington, DC. I was living in the Catholic peace community that became Anne Montgomery House, and she lived at the Sisters of the Holy Child house on Newton Street NE, just three blocks away. The original author stepped back and generously recommended that I take up the project. At Rice's insistence, the scope grew. She showed me that this book *must* be about the larger community of Plowshares, because you can only make sense of one activist by discussing all of them. So with the blessing of Liturgical Press director Peter Dwyer, editor Barry Hudock (who first conceived of this book), editor Stephanie Lancour, and publisher Hans Christoffersen, it now extends to Plowshares more generally.

Rice's life has already been told in rich detail. Especially helpful is *Washington Post* reporter Dan Zak's *Almighty: Courage, Resistance, and Existential Peril in the Nuclear Age*, and I eagerly recommend it.[1] Zak artfully interweaves her story with those of fellow activists Greg Boertje-Obed and Michael Walli, in the context of the growing threat of nuclear weapons. I am grateful to him for meeting with me, returning Rice's papers and other documents he used, and allowing me to compare my original material with his meticulous work.

To understand why this book needed to be broader than others in the "People of God" series, it helps to consider the collective nature of the anti-nuclear movement known as Plowshares. It is not an established organization. Instead, it is a name for a series of interrelated peaceful protest actions at nuclear facilities and military bases that depend on the discernment of a group formed for the purpose. Each disperses after all of its members' prison sentences end. The less visible often do the most to support those in the media spotlight. As Dominican sisters Ardeth Platte (pronounced "Platty") and Carol Gilbert put it, "We always talk about a circle. Everybody in that circle is as important as everybody else. Whether they're home praying, or they're the person that might drive the car, the person that might do support work in prison, they're all part of that circle. Whenever there's a Plowshares action, the media highlights one or two people and then they get all the press. They get all the stories. It goes down that way historically. But it might not even be correct."[2] As longtime Plowshares activist and Catholic Worker Paul Magno said at an event he moderated on the evening of the first day of the Transform Now Plowshares trial, "Lots of people do lots of things to make this hammer fall."[3]

For that reason, this book focuses on the trio known as Transform Now Plowshares. In the very early morning of July 28, 2012, Rice, Boertje-Obed, and Walli entered the Y-12 National Security Complex, a federal nuclear facility at Oak Ridge, Tennessee, which billed itself proudly at the time as "The Fort Knox of Uranium." As veteran Plowshares activist John LaForge commented to the movement's newspaper of record, *The Nuclear Resister*, "Uranium processed [at Y-12] puts the 'H' in our H-bombs."[4] It stores enough of that element to make ten thousand nuclear bombs, and the Y-12 Plowshares action became the largest breach in US nuclear security history. Rice received three years in prison, while Walli and Boertje-Obed received longer sentences of five years. However, just two years later a higher federal court reversed the most serious conviction, for sabotage, and the trial judge released them from any further prison time. It marked an important win for Plowshares in an appeals court.

Although it has been positive for the Plowshares phenomenon generally that Megan Rice is mediagenic, hungry news cycles tended to focus on her for problematic reasons. First, her age (eighty-four when she went to prison in 2014). The words "octogenarian" or "senior citizen" occur in almost all of the coverage from the 2010s. As a *Seattle Times* reporter said of an earlier Plowshares action that directly inspired this one, "It wasn't so much an A-Team, as an AARP Team,"[5] leaving the troubling impression that the older the activist, the more the action is rendered cute rather than serious. Second, stories focused on her gender, as if being a woman makes civil resistance extra newsworthy. And finally, journalists puzzled over her vocation. Catholic sisters can receive objectifying treatment in secular media, with their protests presented either with the cliches of innocence ("a winning smile . . . quiet concern for everyone but herself," went one such description), the mouse that roared ("the notion of an octogenarian nun breaching a high-level nuclear facility guarded by machine guns and tanks"), worthy of condescension ("that young lady there brought a Holy Bible," said congressman at a hearing on the Y-12 incident; "if she had been a terrorist, the Lord only knows what would have happened"), or slap-with-a-ruler ominous.[6]

Journalist and nuclear energy expert Frank Munger noted that the event had made Y-12 an object of humor: "Instead of being compared to the nation's gold standard, Y-12 security was suddenly 'Second to Nun' and the butt of other jokes and slogans."[7] When *New York Times* columnist Nicholas Kristof, who consistently gives Catholic sisters some of their best major media coverage, wrote admiringly that Rice had "masterminded a break-in," she responded, "Plowshares actions strive to be the result of genuine, communal discernment. There can be no 'mastermind.'"[8]

Comedian Carolyn Castiglia, an occasional commenter on HLN Headline News, appeared in a warmhearted segment, defending Rice against a colleague who suggested she wasn't "all there": "No, she's totally all there! Why would she be afraid of prison? Prison is a step up from a convent, you know what I mean? She's used to wearing uniforms, she's used to eating simple meals. She walks into prison, and she's like, 'Oh cool, we can talk here?' I love this lady. She's a fierce feminist. I want to know her."[9] It was a cheerful approach, but it also highlighted why Rice inadvertently got more media than Walli, Boertje-Obed, or most previous activists, and why Transform Now Plowshares became iconic less for the principle of the thing and more for the quirks.

If we can cease thinking of Megan Rice merely as a spunky sister with nothing to lose who raised a ruckus, then we can view all Plowshares activists as they are: principled citizens from various walks of life who make choices according to prayer and the call of their well-formed consciences. To present Transform Now Plowshares in this more accurate context is to leave readers with a much more interesting (and perhaps terrifying) possibility: what if any of us might be called to do something this risky and bold?

Does this mean all of us should participate in a Plowshares protest action? It is difficult to speculate, because Plowshares isn't quite like anything else, not even twentieth-century movements such as Dorothy Day and Peter Maurin's Catholic Worker, Catherine Doherty's Madonna House apostolate, or the disrupt-the-Vietnam-draft actions of the Baltimore Four and the Catonsville Nine—the latter burning draft records with homemade napalm in a Maryland parking lot—from which it arose most directly. Plowshares has surely been controversial even among peace activists who debate it vigorously. It disturbs people.

But then, so did John the Baptist.

Speaking of prophets, it is notable that even though global people of faith disagree endlessly about what constitutes scripture, the books of Isaiah and Micah from which Plowshares takes its name aren't controversial. The two prophets are venerated among many major religions: Catholic, Protestant, and Orthodox Christianity; Mormonism; Judaism; and Islam. So when we read Isaiah 2:4—"they shall beat their swords into plowshares, and their spears into pruning hooks: nation shall not lift up sword against nation, neither shall they learn war any more"—and Micah 4:3—"He shall judge between many peoples, and shall arbitrate between strong nations far away; they shall beat their swords into plowshares, and their spears into pruning hooks; nation shall not lift up sword against nation, neither shall they learn war any more"—let us bear in mind that *most people of faith in the world* understand these passages as being relevant to our own lives and times. As Ardeth Platte commented, "When two prophets do the commissioning, it is very relevant."[10]

So, given that a majority of the religious world believes a sword somewhere must eventually find its way into the form of a plowshare for Isaiah and Micah to be fulfilled, then if not nuclear weapons, what?

If not now, when?

And if not us, who?

Carole Sargent

Acknowledgments

There have been scores of Plowshares actions in many countries—the United States, Ireland, the Netherlands, Italy, Germany, Australia, New Zealand, Sweden, and Great Britain—and the actions now span more than forty years. Jack and Felice Cohen-Joppa, who together edit *The Nuclear Resister*; Art Laffin of DC's Dorothy Day Catholic Worker; formerly imprisoned activist Susan Crane; and the late Sr. Anne Montgomery have chronicled Plowshares and related disarmament actions since the first one in 1980. They estimate there have been about 101 as of 2021. Not everyone involved with Plowshares has done so out of a biblical faith conviction, but many have, and many of the secular ones—whether they called themselves Plowshares or not—were inspired by it.

Abundant thanks go to so many who advised on this book, gave interviews, corrected errors, and calibrated my understanding. Thanks are especially due to (alphabetically) Jackie Allen-Douçot of the Hartford Catholic Worker; John Amidon of Veterans For Peace; Mary Lou Anderson of the Western Shoshone Nation; Quaker chaplain John Bach of Harvard; Ellen Barfield of Veterans For Peace; Anne Bennis of Trident Nein Plowshares; Frida Berrigan; Willa Bickham of Viva House; Chief Johnnie Bobb of the Western Shoshone

Nation; Greg Boertje-Obed of the Duluth Catholic Worker; Kathy Boylan of the Dorothy Day Catholic Worker; Roy Bourgeois of SOA Watch; Ken Butigan of DePaul University; Carolyn Castiglia; Drew Christensen, SJ, of Georgetown University; Jeanne Clark, OP, of Homecoming Farm; Dennis Coday of the *National Catholic Reporter*; Felice and Jack Cohen-Joppa of *The Nuclear Resister*; Mark Colville of the Kings Bay Plowshares 7; Kathleen Conan, RSCJ; Frank Cordaro of the Des Moines Catholic Worker; Susan Crane of Disarm Now Plowshares; Fr. John Dear of the Beatitudes Center for the Nonviolent Jesus; Virginia Dennehy, RSCJ; Anabel Dwyer of the Lawyers Committee on Nuclear Policy; David Eberhardt of the Baltimore Four; Lydia Essien, a former Holy Child student in Nigeria; Megan Finnerty; Sue and Bill Frankel-Streit; Michael Gallagher; Judith Garson, RSCJ; Carol Gilbert, OP, of the Dorothy Day Catholic Worker; Clare Grady of the Kings Bay Plowshares 7; Kathleen Guinan of Crossway Community; Ryan Hall of Pace e Bene; Bill Hartman of Trident Nein Plowshares; Martha Hennessy of the Kings Bay Plowshares 7; Ralph Hutchison of the Oak Ridge Environmental Peace Alliance; Kathy Kelly of Voices for Creative Nonviolence; Nancy Kehoe, RSCJ; Steve Kelly, SJ, of the Kings Bay Plowshares 7; musician Charlie King; Plowshares lawyer Blake Kremer; Art Laffin of the Dorothy Day Catholic Worker; John LaForge of Nukewatch; Rachel Maddow of MSNBC; Paul Magno of Jonah House and the Dorothy Day Catholic Worker; Rick Massimo of WTOP Radio; Lissa McLeod of Dragonfly Aerial Arts Studio; Pat McSweeney; Michele Naar-Obed of the Duluth Catholic Worker; Martin Newell, CP, of the London Catholic Worker; Mary Novak of NETWORK and the Georgetown University Law Center; Patrick O'Neill of the Kings Bay Plowshares 7; Carolyn Osiek, RSCJ Archivist;

Julia Occhiogrosso of the Las Vegas Catholic Worker; Libby Pappalardo of the Creech Fourteen; Michael Pera, Assistant RSCJ Archivist; Tim Pettolina; Ardeth Platte, OP, of the Dorothy Day Catholic Worker; Clare Pratt, RSCJ, of Anne Montgomery House; lawyer Bill Quigley; Timothy Quinn of the Trident Nein Plowshares; Megan Rice, SHCJ; Rosalie Riegle of the Catholic Worker extended family; Diane Roche, RSCJ of Anne Montgomery House; Molly Rush of the Plowshares Eight; Br. Javier Del Ángel De los Santos, OFM; John Schuchardt of the Plowshares Eight; Bob Schwartz, working with Ramsey Clark; Christopher Spicer; Paula Toner, RSCJ; Megan Hooke Tourlis; Mary Evelyn Tucker and John Grim of the Yale Forum on Religion and Ecology; Sergio Vasquez; Anne Wachter, RSCJ; Michael Walli of the Dorothy Day Catholic Worker; Brendan Walsh of Viva House; Mindy Werner; Paki Wieland of CodePink; Kim Williams and Steve Baggarly of the Norfolk Catholic Worker; Colonel Ann Wright of Veterans For Peace; Helen Young, director of *The Nuns, The Priests, and The Bombs*; and Dan Zak of *The Washington Post*.

So yes, in keeping with Liturgical Press's *People of God* series, this book began with the life of one Catholic sister, but now it is an account of the journey of many activists. This is a narrative of their collective story, one that continues to unfold into the twenty-first century.

PLOWSHARES SACRAMENTS: "EVERY MOVEMENT OF OUR BODY WAS A LITURGY"

After anti-nuclear activist Sr. Ardeth Platte died on September 30, 2020, members of the Dorothy Day Catholic Worker held her memorial service in her garden. The coronavirus pandemic was in full roar, which meant no big funeral, but this was a cloudless October morning and a lovely time to gather outdoors at least six feet apart and masked. Veteran Plowshares activist Kathy Boylan, who lived in the same community, created an altar featuring Platte's hammer, a pair of bolt cutters, and a coil of crime scene tape. One of her friends that day brought sunflowers in a vase and placed them to the left. Beside them sat a basket of white roses. Michael Walli also grew sunflowers that dotted the garden, now at the end of their season.

Plowshares is visual and, arguably, liturgical. When Platte had described how she and fellow Dominican sisters Carol Gilbert and Jackie Hudson had approached the silo of a Minuteman missile to hammer on it and paint a cross in their own blood, she said, "Every movement of our body was a liturgy."[1] Art Laffin continues this image: "For me, the actions that I have been part of were deeply spiritual, even sacramental."[2] Megan Rice agreed, "Oh, it was totally a liturgy. That's why we went in, you know, to prayerfully be at the site. And expose and oppose what was happening there. And you know, in the name of the mind and heart of God, and for restoring justice to our planet. Not only to our country, but to our planet. Restore the possibility of the value of justice reigning on the earth, which is the kingdom of God."[3]

Daniel Berrigan wrote, in his 1982 book Portraits of Those I Love, "We do not stand there to play God or to form a theater of cruelty or absurdity. Our acts are simply extensions of the sacraments (baptism, eucharist), celebrations of the liturgical year (Ash Wednesday, Good Friday, Easter, Holy Innocents)."[4]

Bill Frankel-Streit is a former priest now married to fellow activist Sue Frankel-Streit. Before they were married, they participated in the ANZUS (Australia/New Zealand/United States) Plowshares action in 1991. They entered Griffiss Air Force Base in Rome, New York, choosing a day just before the bombers made airstrikes on Iraq, considering such strikes "blasphemous." When asked about actions in this context, he replied, "It's like any sacrament. How do you gauge the effectiveness? Well, you don't. How do you gauge the effectiveness of Eucharist? You don't. You just surrender to it, and trust and have faith that something is happening. As Dan Berrigan said, 'We do what is right, just, and good, and leave the results in the hands greater than ours.' Which is what any sacrament is about."[5]

CHAPTER ONE

A Gifted Life

Megan Rice—her first name is pronounced "MEE-gan"—mused late in life that if she were ever to write her memoir, she would title it *A Gifted Life*.[1] She felt her parents provided a beautiful and rich early formation, putting her on a clear path to her seventy-plus-year vocation with the Society of the Holy Child Jesus. Born January 31, 1930, in the midst of the Great Depression, Rice would refer many years later to that timing in her own court trial. It gave her an opening to address poverty and inequality, something the judge, in an effort to maintain focus on what the government considered to be the facts of the case, tried to forbid.

The Catholics of Morningside Heights

Megan's mother, Dr. Madeleine Hooke Rice, would seem accomplished and progressive by early twenty-first century standards, let alone in the 1930s. She went to Barnard College, where Margaret Mead was a classmate, and earned a master's and doctorate from Columbia University. She became a professor at Hunter College in an era when only

about four percent of women finished college. Her dissertation, *American Catholic Opinion in the Slavery Controversy*, was the first study of its kind. It was later published
by Columbia University Press.[2] Madeleine was deeply influenced by the thought and example of Catherine de Hueck
Doherty, who founded an apostolate called Friendship
House in the 1930s to foster interracial understanding at a
time when most of the country was segregated. When Megan
was a child, the Rice family attended Friendship House
meetings regularly.

As for her father, she says with a starchy practicality that
he "studied and taught the rhythm method."[3] This mildly
spicy description doesn't begin to sum up the career of Dr.
Frederick W. Rice, a graduate of Holy Cross and Columbia,
who was head of obstetrics at New York City's Bellevue
Hospital and professor of obstetrics at New York University
Medical School. After his medical internship, he was in the
"Fighting Irish" regiment of the New York National Guard
and worked during World War I as a surgeon. He was also
a lay member of a family life committee for the New York
Archdiocese.[4] His work as an obstetrician helped Megan
become aware of the life circumstances of a wide range of
women who lived the reality of different levels of healthcare
available depending on race, class, gender, and religion.

Consistent with his wife's advocacy of African-American
civil rights through her dissertation and book, he published
on health disparities, noting the disproportionate number
of women of color who died in childbirth each year because
of lack of access to medical facilities. He was well-known
for his pamphlet, "Regarding Recent Efforts to Reduce Mortality in Childbirth," which contended that trained nurse-
midwives could manage births anywhere but especially in
rural or underprivileged areas with inadequate access to

doctors.[5] His work on better healthcare for the marginalized sounds essential today, but back then not everyone was cheering. An uncle returning from a visit to Bangor asked, "How many times did I have to think of an answer when they said, 'Freddie Rice is a communist!'"[6]

Megan was Madeleine and Frederick's third child. She had two older sisters, Alessandra and Madeleine, the latter named for their mother and known as Maddy.

There is a story attached to the unusual pronunciation of Megan's first name. One day during her pregnancy, Madeleine read aloud from the newspaper that British politician Lloyd George had a daughter named Megan, who had recently become the first female member of Parliament for Wales. What a perfect choice for a baby name, she commented. They assumed the Welsh pronunciation would have been "MEE-gan" (although old Pathé newsreels suggest that it was in fact "MEG-an"), and the charming pronunciation stuck. It has continued in family tradition for a niece and grandniece, and they are known affectionately within the family as Megan #1, Megan #2, and Megan #3.

Megan's parents were part of the intellectual Catholic left that flourished in the Morningside Heights area of upper Manhattan. It was nicknamed the "Academic Acropolis" for its abundant campuses such as Columbia University, Barnard College, the Jewish Theological Seminary of America, Union Theological Seminary, and many more.[7] Then and today it holds the highest percentage of college-educated residents in New York City and has always been tweedily upper middle class, meaning that it boasts more intellectual cachet than sheer wealth. The Rice family attended Mass at Corpus Christi Church near Columbia University. The pastor was Fr. George Barry Ford, a well-known liberal firebrand who frequently publicly disagreed with (and was twice silenced by) Cardinal Francis Spellman. When the Columbia graduate student Thomas Merton decided in 1938 that he wished to enter the Roman Catholic Church, he sought out Fr. Ford.

Frederick and Madeleine's friends and acquaintances during Megan's childhood were something of a Catholic who's-who of the era. She remembers visits from social justice advocates Dorothy Day, Peter Maurin, and Catherine de Hueck Doherty; Catholic book publishers Frank Sheed and Maisie Ward; the English Dominican historian Fr. Bede Jarrett; and Fr. John Monaghan, one of the founders of the Labor College at Fordham University.

Rice remembers Day speaking "very gravely" with her mother Madeleine, who would have provided financial support and then connected Day to other affluent Catholic friends. She remembers Day as, "an intense person, someone with the heritage of the age on her shoulders."[8] The ideas and events covered by Day and Maurin's newspaper, *The Catholic Worker*, were frequent topics of discussion in the home.

Rice remembers one occasion when Sheed and Ward—who were known, in addition for having published some of the most important Catholic works of the day, also for their lively street debates in London—engaged in vigorous conversation with an interracial group of Catholic high school students from Harlem in a large room of the Rice apartment. "Frank Sheed or Maisie Ward would heckle these young people," Rice recalled, "the way they had been heckled on the streets of London."[9] The couple pushed the students to defend the faith, but it was done in good humor and with warmth and affection.

It's hard these days to imagine having to learn how to "defend" Roman Catholic doctrine, because the belligerence it faced then from many non-Catholics has been replaced by indifference, although some remain vocally hostile. But in the late 1930s and early 1940s—before the popularity of television personality Fulton J. Sheen, the literary triumphs of Flannery O'Connor and Thomas Merton, the widespread fascination with John and Jacqueline Kennedy in the White House, and the Second Vatican Council of the mid-1960s made Catholicism more familiar to mainline Protestants—being publicly Catholic could mean difficulty in finding a job or even living where one wished.

As Megan's knowledge of science increased, she became aware of the career of the scientist across the hall. She grew up with the daughters of Dr. Selig Hecht, a biophysics professor at Columbia University, whom she came to suspect but could never prove was involved in the Manhattan Project, the research and development group that made the first atomic bombs. To hear Rice remember it, Hecht's work was so top-secret that he could not tell even his wife or children. Megan asked her parents why such secrecy was necessary, but never received a satisfying answer. As a believer in community discernment who was distrustful of obfuscation, she said many decades later, "I think my enlightenment came from the fact that if something were good, he wouldn't have to keep it secret."[10]

Hecht died of a heart attack at age fifty-five, in 1947, shortly after publishing *Explaining the Atom*, a book for general readers that sold widely. Rice was seventeen at the time and had already decided to become a Catholic sister, which she did later the same year. When Madeleine told her daughters of Hecht's death, she added, "He asked if his ashes could be sprinkled over the Pacific."[11] This struck Megan as peculiar. It would send a strong message . . . but about *what* exactly? Did it reference what happened at Hiroshima and Nagasaki? In his book he claimed he never worked directly on those bombs, but today Rice feels certain he must have, although she offers no direct evidence. She would ruminate about Hecht for the rest of her life, often out loud to friends and even on one occasion in court, insistent that his secret activities were a spur for spending her later years resisting nuclear weapons.

Madeleine Hooke Rice's younger brother Walter Hooke was also a driving force for Rice's later activism. Hooke joined the Marines three days after Pearl Harbor and was stationed in Japan after the war. Deeply Catholic like the rest of his family, Hooke attended Mass whenever military duties permitted, and he befriended the Bishop of Nagasaki, Paul Aijirō Yamaguchi, who happened to be away when the city was bombed and thus was spared. Hooke helped Bishop Yamaguchi crawl through the ruin of the cathedral about a month after the bombing, looking for items to save. Bishop Yamaguchi gave him a gift: a large, wooden cross that had adorned the altar.

Her uncle's stories of the aftermath of Nagasaki affected Megan Rice profoundly. She believed he had post-traumatic stress disorder. Rather than retreat into his own pain, however, he worked to help other veterans. He identified as a worker and became an activist in solidarity with other workers, befriending César Chávez personally and participating in the California grape boycotts in the late 1960s.

Hooke's business card had "Listen to the voices of your people" printed on the front, and the Association of Catholic Trade Unionists' Prayer of the Worker on the back. He loved Jesus most in his human identity as a carpenter. Another version of Hooke's card bore the same passage from the book of Isaiah that animates the activists in this book: "They shall beat their swords into plowshares and their spears into pruning hooks; One nation shall not raise the sword against another, nor shall they train for war again" (2:4). Hooke later worked tirelessly to support the Radiation-Exposed Veterans Compensation Act of 1988, fighting for benefits for veterans who developed cancers related to their work with atomic bombing and tests. He also joined groups including the National Association of Atomic Veterans, National Association of Radiation Survivors, Disabled American Veterans, the American Legion, and the Veterans of Foreign Wars.

When Hooke spoke at the First Global Radiation Victims Conference in 1987, he recalled living through the aftermath of the bomb in Nagasaki. He was impressed by the Nuremberg trials, where Allied forces held Germany's leaders responsible for Nazi war crimes. He called for a Nuremberg-style trial against United States leaders who had knowingly subjected soldiers to radiation and done nothing to warn or protect them. Hooke described with horror a US military football game played on New Years' Day 1946 in Nagasaki. This "Atom Bowl Game" was played on ground poisoned by an atomic blast less than five months earlier. Hooke wondered if the Marines thought their men would have revolted or refused to serve if they had understood what radiation exposure meant. Instead, leaders lied to their own troops and let the game proceed. In ignorance, soldiers drank local water from a contaminated reservoir and went postwar sightseeing in the heavily radiated district around the bombed cathedral, about five hundred yards from Ground Zero.

Hooke kept the cross from Bishop Yamaguchi in his dining room until 1982, when he donated it to Wilmington College's Peace Resources Center, in Ohio. Decades later, the institution returned it to Joseph Mitsuaki Takami, the Archbishop of Nagasaki, and Megan Rice was interviewed for a feature about it by NHK, the Japanese television equivalent of PBS.

Each of the Rice daughters attended St. Walburga's Academy of the Society of the Holy Child at Riverside Drive and 140th Street (now The School of the Holy Child and relocated to Rye, New York). Their parents could not possibly have anticipated how much of an influence this choice would have on the girls. Imagine their surprise when in 1945, after just one year at Barnard, Alessandra announced she was leaving college to become a Holy Child sister. This might have been welcome news to many traditional Catholic parents, but for an academic like Madeleine Rice, it was deeply concerning, at least at first, because she had such high academic hopes for her daughters, and she had envisioned being a very happy grandmother to their children. She felt better after she got to know the novice mistress, Mother Laurentia Dalton. Already at the time, Dalton was known to the Society of the Holy Child Jesus (SHCJ) as "our pioneer," because in 1930 she had become the first North American SHCJ in Africa. Along with their superior general and two sisters from England, Mother Dalton launched their first teacher-training schools in the port city of Calabar, Nigeria, which would become one of the most important sites for women's education in that nation. She spoke so knowledgeably with Megan's father about urgent maternity problems in Nigeria that he and Madeleine came to fully accept these sisters as global, educated, erudite women who were also deeply prayerful.

When, two years later, seventeen-year-old Megan shared the news that she, too, planned to enter the SHCJ, Madeleine was exasperated. Though not quite as dismayed as she had initially been with the similar announcement from Alessandra, she called out, half to her daughters and half in Hamlet-like soliloquy, "What am I turning out to be? A nursery for the Holy Child order?"[12]

And thus in 1947 Megan Rice became Sr. Frederick Mary. The congregation chose the name for her, to honor her father. Afterward, everyone called her "Sr. Freddie" until the early 1970s, when she put aside the habit and became Sr. Megan Rice once again.

PLOWSHARES SACRAMENTS: SUNFLOWERS

Sunflowers are symbols in the disarmament community throughout the world. They have a history and function in the nuclear conversation going back to the earliest days of the technology. As "hyperaccumulators," they have a remarkable ability to leach heavy metals out of soil. Other plants such as field mustard, pigweed, and cockscomb can do similar jobs, but the sunflower is inexpensive, easy to find, propagates quickly, and creates a satisfyingly glorious sea of color. At Chernobyl in Russia, site of a catastrophic nuclear accident in 1986, sunflowers extracted cesium 137 and strontium 90 from the ground. Acres of them wave at the site of Japan's 2011 Fukushima Daiichi disaster.

Some activists, such as the five members of Disarm Now Plowshares—Susan Crane, Lynne Greenwald, Sr. Anne Montgomery, and the Jesuits Steve Kelly and Bill Bichsel—who entered Naval Base Kitsap-Bangor's strategic weapons facility in 2009, have sprinkled sunflower seeds during their protest actions. The Disarm Now Plowshares group has even sold "Father Bix Anti-Nuke Sunflower Seeds" as a witty fundraiser. In their official statement, they wrote, "We bring sunflower seeds to plant the hope of new life in this violated earth."[13] Others bring the flowers themselves, distribute them to employees at the site, or paint them on banners and posters.

Peace activist and author Kathy Kelly, who founded Voices for Creative Nonviolence, remembers a group called the Missouri Peace Planters planting sunflowers in the earth at nuclear missile silos. They also planted corn, "noting land was meant to grow corn and wheat and not to harbor weapons of mass destruction."[14] Protesters have also at times planted trees.

The Ground Zero Center for Nonviolent Action's logo depicts a nuclear missile broken in half by a sunflower, symbolizing the power of nonviolence. The newsletter of the Nuclear Age Peace Foundation is called The Sunflower.

An Exceptional Education

Because Megan Rice grew up in a medical household and had always loved science and animals, biology seemed an obvious major, and she was gratified that her superiors agreed. In 1957 she graduated from Villanova with a bachelor's degree in secondary school biology, at a time when fewer than 4 percent of women earned bachelor's degrees.[15] Master's degrees were highly unusual for women in the 1950s, with just 385 women in the whole nation earning one in her field of biology. She completed a master's in radioactive biology at Boston College, in conjunction with work at Harvard Medical School. Because the ministers of education in Nigeria had been to Oxford and Cambridge, and their school system was British, they generally didn't recognize degrees from some of the Catholic universities in the United States such as Villanova, Marymount, or the Holy Child sisters' own Rosemont, where she did some of her studies. Rice needed a more readily known international brand, so Father Sullivan, head of the biology department at Boston College, invited her to become a graduate student researcher. She spent long hours at the microscope, counting dots, following tracer elements, and studying causes of cancer. Dan Zak notes the striking image of her wearing a lead vest over her full habit, for protection.[16] All of this awakened her earliest interest in nuclear radiation. She also attended what was then called "normal school" to certify as an elementary school science teacher, amassing credits slowly throughout the early 1950s while busy teaching science at Holy Child high schools. She recalls working with the Harvard medical team to write to Eastman Kodak for radioactive tritium. It had to be kept in total darkness, in a deep freeze. As she learned how cells become cancerous, she thought and she prayed.

She earned her master's degree in May 1962 and left for Nigeria that summer. She had dreamed of Africa ever since being in Mother Laurentia Dalton's class and hearing those wonderful stories, and it was her sole request when entering the Society. She was deeply content with her assignment and spent the next forty years essentially happy. She didn't return, except for rare visits, until 2003, although she came back a bit more often toward the end for medical treatments. That means she experienced everything from the Kennedy and King assassinations to the turmoil of the sixties to Watergate to Iran-Contra and Chernobyl to the first Gulf War as an expatriate, listening to the crackly BBC World Service on shortwave radio. Many common touchstones such as sixties culture, flower children, British invasion rock, and so many iconic big-screen movies went right past her. Her dear friend Pat McSweeney has often called her "Rip Van Winkle" because she was out of the country so long.[17]

> *"Holy Spirit and W-H-O-L-L-Y spirit."*
> *Megan Rice*[18]

Education is one key ministry of the Holy Child congregation, and in Africa they developed teacher training colleges that turned into formal secondary schools, which remain in operation to this day. When Rice arrived in Africa, she was assigned to the Handmaid of the Holy Child Jesus, a one-year-old boarding school, then known as a "convent school" or a "bush school," in a rural area of coastal Nigeria (it later moved to a better site farther inland called Abakaliki).[19] Locals sometimes described the original site as better suited as the abode of lizards and birds rather than young learners.[20] There was no electricity or water in the compound. The sisters had to sleep in mosquito-infested classrooms at night.

Religious education was part of the core curriculum in most of English-speaking Africa, and students could choose either Catholic or Protestant Christianity, or one of their Native traditions. This compromise bridged a strong rivalry between Catholics and Protestants that continues, especially in the southern part of Nigeria. Rice recalled that about 45 percent of the students chose a Catholic formation, 45 percent Protestant, and 10 percent traditional African. She engaged with Muslims and their imams, who listened to her out of courtesy and gradually developed a dialogue with those in the Catholic faith.

Rice taught in Nigeria for thirty-five years, in a progressive religious education program, working with the nation's Ministry of Education. During that time, she also gave short workshops for twenty to thirty teachers at a time, in tandem with another Catholic sister and a Presbyterian laywoman, who together became her two most trusted teaching partners.

The Nigerian girls who attended the Holy Child school were fortunate, though not all wealthy, because they came from families with the vision to support their education. They may not have seemed rich by Western standards at the time, but thanks to their families' foresight and willingness to encourage their daughters' intellectual development, these girls had outstanding opportunities. Many of Rice's former students went into the teaching profession. Some became education administrators, often working for state governments and ensuring the future of women's education in Nigeria.

While the high school girls were eager to learn, the sisters had to work harder to recruit elementary school children, because the idea of educating younger girls broke with tradition at the time. "We had to nurture their parents," Rice remembers. Within a decade all of this changed, as the government began to appoint teachers in the late 1960s and early 1970s. Education became more of a national priority, and the country embarked on a path that would lead to rapid development. Today Nigeria has a global reputation for education, and it's hard to recall a time when it wasn't as much of a priority. Life in Nigeria then was very different from what she knew in the United States. Sisters rose at 5:00 a.m. (Rice still does) and prayed alone. Mass was usually at 6:00. Then came breakfast and morning classes, which went until 1:00 p.m. They didn't even have a telephone pole until her second year in Nigeria, when the Saint Patrick Fathers installed one for their parish and secondary school. Rice and her mother wrote to each other every week, though it would take up to two weeks for each letter to arrive.

The sisters hired local carpenters to make student desks, but they had to build the first one as a prototype, because Nigerian laborers in the early 1960s had never seen one. Those sisters weren't skillful carpenters, but they nevertheless did it excitedly, holding in their hearts a sense of privilege and opportunity to fill the classrooms with desks and have the chance to teach something new.

Rice also designed the work tables in her biology lab. Throughout graduate school she had taught math, chemistry, and biology part-time at a high school in Melrose, Massachusetts, so she felt at least reasonably prepared to teach a broader range of algebra, geometry, biology, and general science. She developed her leadership skills, and over the years she sometimes served as principal or vice-principal whenever it was necessary, though she claims that such roles don't come naturally to her.

New sisters arriving in the Nigerian missions felt like true foreigners at first. They struggled to eat the pounded yam with groundnut soup or boiled rice with palm kernel sauce that were typical of the local diet. Some sisters wondered aloud how the local people could eat such bland fare every day. However, *oyibo* food—foreign dishes that white people eat— was not readily available in Nigeria at the time. Eventually the sisters did more than just tolerate the local food. Many grew to love and even crave it.

In all cultures, food is deeply integrated with human relationships, and Rice knew from day one that their engagement with African cuisine wasn't just about the diet. "You learn to appreciate varieties of ways of eating, ways of being insulted or insulting, ways of relating with respect, and [adapting to] the clothing, the colors," she recalled. "Sometimes the children would burst out laughing, even at a meal, but I didn't realize it was in admiration. Laughing in America can seem as though you're laughing at the person. But this was a way of showing admiration, and it took me a while, because nobody interpreted that for us."[21]

Grade levels of students within classrooms were more mixed than in most US schools, with some first and second grades put together and up to forty girls in a single classroom. The custom at the time was to teach rote memorization of the Bible, but Rice and her companions promoted a new mode of teaching that was more dialogue-based and life-centered.

Brazilian educator Paulo Freire's 1968 book (published in English in 1970), *Pedagogy of the Oppressed*,[22] was nearly ubiquitous in Catholic education in the seventies; it became a core text not just for the SHCJ in Africa, but for many progressive Catholic sisters worldwide. Instead of thinking of their duty as changing their African students, the sisters approached each subject, whether biology or chemistry or geography, by listening to the children and helping them become co-creators of their own educational outcomes. Although Rice was still the teacher and always maintained order, she understood teaching as a form of friendship. She followed the prescribed curriculum set forth by the government, but in a personal way that for her was also her form of ministry.

When Rice arrived in Nigeria, women religious were held in great respect, and she felt safe there. Rice said local women offered to wash the sisters' clothing, either in wash tubs or down at the river. She was concerned about having them do too much, especially when the girls had to walk close to a mile to bring back a bucket of water. Eventually the sisters agreed to raise the money to dig a well.

At six o'clock in the morning on December 11, 1963, Rice—who had been in Nigeria now for about eighteen months—was accompanying her fellow sisters at the boarding school into Mass. One of them approached her and told her that they had just received bad news about her sister Alessandra, a teacher at Rosemont College in Philadelphia whose name in religious life was Cornelia Augusta. She had died suddenly, at age thirty-seven, of a genetic disorder called Marfan syndrome. Alessandra had been with some of her students just the evening before, joking and laughing.

Rice remembers that the introit, the first prayer in the Mass, was Psalm 21:2, "You have granted him his heart's desire; you did not refuse the request of his lips."[23] She interpreted it as a sign that Alessandra was with her and that she had gotten "her heart's desire." "My first reaction," she recalled, "is, 'Now she's here.'"

In those days a sister was not permitted to fly home for funerals, so she simply had to deal with the loss without joining her family.

"It was stunning," she recalled. "It was really stunning. But I think I had a grace, because I always felt badly that she couldn't go to Africa and I could. I was much younger, four years younger. Even my middle sister felt badly for the older one, because I got there but we both wanted to go. I felt I had out-sprinted her."[24]

Ghana

Throughout the middle and later years of the 1960s, a political and ethnic conflict brewed in Nigeria. One day Rice and several other sisters were navigating in a long canoe up a river into Cameroon when they observed a single plane flying overhead in the same direction. While soldiers on the shore shot at it, the plane dropped what she supposed were homemade bombs into the water. They didn't make a big enough explosion to be really threatening—in fact, she and the sisters, including her close friend the Reverend Mother, actually laughed nervously. It was also quite a sight to watch soldiers using common shotguns to try to bring down an airplane.

Finally, in 1968, a civil war began. The sisters were optimistic it would end soon, but then the state ordered all children home from boarding school. At first, the sisters assumed their students would return in a few months, but it soon became evident that they weren't coming back. Finally, the government ordered the sisters out, along with all expatriates, because it was no longer safe in the country. A few students remained at the school sites, but only for lack of anywhere else to go, to live there and wait out the war.

During this hiatus, Rice first went to England, and then visited the United States before returning to teach in Ghana until the Nigerian war ended. Reuniting with her fellow sisters there was wonderful but also heartbreaking—they learned that two of the Nigerian school's students had been killed, and there was great mourning for them. Although they expected it wouldn't last, she ended up teaching in Ghana for six years.

The war was an enormous disruption to the girls' education, but Rice remembers a heartening story. While the sisters were away, the older girls taught the younger ones. During one opportunity that Rice had to visit Abakaliki during the conflict, she saw a girl working geometry on the blackboard, using a unique visual method that Rice recognized as her own. When she asked the student where she learned to do it, she replied that a senior taught her. Rice recognized the girl she named as a former student. In this way the girls who loved learning grew up more quickly, with an energy and passion for teaching and learning that made Rice confident that they could and would continue with or without the sisters. Perhaps somewhere today a teacher stands at a blackboard in Africa who wasn't even born yet when Rice left, but nevertheless teaches geometry using that unique style.[25]

If Rice had remained in New York, the dramatic 1968 Columbia University protests—which include the occupation of many campus buildings by students and the violent removal of protesters by the New York City Police Department—would have been right on her doorstep. The protests centered, like so many across the United States at the time, on the Vietnam War. She mourned and regretted that conflict. However, unlike many of her present-day Plowshares colleagues who watched the daily news coverage of what would come to be known as the first televised war, she experienced it from Africa with a bit more intellectual and emotional distance.

Instead, African realities, like Nigeria's severance of its ties to Britain, the Nigerian Civil War, the concurrent famine in the former Republic of Biafra, coups and counter-coups, were her foreground. She also learned more about US atrocities, particularly in Latin America, since that news was disseminated abroad more fully than in the United States, and non-US journalists tended to believe it more.

* * *

While in Africa, Rice began one of her longest-lasting friendships. She met Fr. Pierre Samson, who became her spiritual director during her sabbatical to East Africa in 1976, when he taught Scripture to a group of retreatants in Eldoret, Kenya. Later he visited the diocese in her region of Nigeria to give workshops on "Gospel Sharing," and they bonded. Samson was a Canadian, Québécois member of the Prêtres des Missions-Étrangères (PME), a missionary congregation. Though he was nearly twenty years her junior, they felt like kindred spirits and started corresponding by letter, an ongoing exchange that would last until his death in 2016.

In the early 1980s, Rice also met and began corresponding with Dr. Seymour Melman, an industrial engineering professor at Columbia University who by that time had been a central figure in the anti-war and disarmament movements for nearly two decades. She attended some of his teach-ins, including one in 1982 at New York's Riverside Church. The term "teach-in" was common in the sixties, seventies, and eighties as a way to describe a looser teacher-student relationship and more fluid time boundaries, with outsiders welcome to a teaching experience that became more like an open social event, usually focused on social justice and effected change through dialogue. Besides teaching, activists also held "pray-ins" (for example, outside the White House) or "die-ins" (at war protests). Melman was an outspoken advocate of what he called "economic conversion," creating jobs by transforming nuclear sites around the world into facilities for other uses for the good of humankind. He chaired a group called the National Commission for Economic Conversion and Disarmament. In her testimony during her 2013 trial for the Y-12 action, Rice would attribute the word *Transform* in the name of the "Transform Now Plowshares" to Melman's influence.

Today, we're much more sensitive to the appearance of colonialism, but even in the late sixties and early seventies, Rice and her religious congregation could identify some of the troubling implications of their work. As the years progressed, she also wanted to step out of the way of younger African protégés who could and should take her place in leadership. She left the ministry of education confident the work would go on appropriately.

Although she had been thinking about retiring from that role for a while, Rice's health finally forced her to leave Africa. Just as it had affected Mother Laurentia Dalton decades earlier, Rice struggled with malaria, a malady that returned to their community periodically and also claimed many African lives. "You ache all over," she recalled, "and there are so many [unpleasant] remedies."[26]

Rice went back and forth between Africa and New York toward the end of her time there. She returned permanently to the United States in 2003, but her African experience never left her. Today she delights in meeting natives of Nigeria and Ghana in the Washington, DC, area. "So many have [doctorates or medical degrees] who can't use them here," she laments. "Some are also pastors." If she thinks she recognizes a name or an accent, she's almost always right, and sometimes she says a few words to the surprised person in their local language. Beautiful conversations have followed, and some become so nostalgic that they don't want her to leave. It is common to see one of these encounters conclude with sentimental tears and a spontaneous, long hug.

As positive as her experience was, she seems equivocal on whether anyone should go to Africa today as she did. Young people could go for their own enrichment, and teaching is always a good idea whether here or abroad, but she thinks Nigeria and Ghana no longer need the help she offered. "Now," she notes with delight, it is a "regular, normal thing [for everyone] to go to secondary school."[27]

PLOWSHARES SACRAMENTS: BREAD

Megan Rice remembers something a bit spontaneous and inspired at a memorial Mass. As she distributed Communion, she offered the host to a grieving friend. After she said, "Body of Christ," as in the standard Catholic Mass, the communicant whispered back, "You are the body of Christ."[28] She agrees, believing that all people of faith become the body of God in the bread, and she calls herself and all of us to live the meaning of Eucharist in the world.

Bread in its everyday sense is an inherent part of protest culture, especially in the 1970s. Daniel Berrigan famously escaped the FBI after a speech at Cornell University in 1970 by hiding in a costume of the Bread and Puppet the-

ater costume—a Vermont-based theater organization known for creating community by sharing free fresh bread with the audience at each performance—and mingling with the group. Back then the word bread was a slang term for money. In the loaves-and-fishes sense, it inspired the name of a California anti-nuclear group, Bread Not Bombs, which merged in the 1980s into the larger Food Not Bombs movement.

Bread seems so harmless. At an appeal for Transform Now Plowshares, when the prosecutor accused them of interfering with national defense, Circuit Judge Raymond Kethledge—who wrote the majority opinion overturning their sabotage conviction—was incredulous, responding, "With a loaf of bread?"[29]

Writing from Danbury Prison where she served time in 2021 for the Kings Bay Plowshares action, Martha Hennessy, a granddaughter of Dorothy Day and a longtime volunteer at Maryhouse Catholic Worker in New York City, contemplates John 6:31:

'My father gives you the true bread from heaven. For the bread of God is that which comes down from heaven, and gives life to the world.'

This inspires us to discern what is from God and what is from man.

What does it mean to believe the very body of Christ will feed the hungry and thirsty?

When we eat this bread of Eucharistic resistance and we trust in the Mystical body of Christ, and our baptized eyes are opened wide to the trickery of man's self-reliance, then our path becomes both a terrible challenge and a great inspiration.[30]

CHAPTER TWO

New Life in Nevada

After decades in sun-drenched west-central Africa, Megan Rice found that she could no longer tolerate New York winters; the city's noise and relentless activity were also foreign to her now. Welcoming the opportunity for a warmer climate and slower pace, Rice received permission from her superiors in 2003 to relocate to Las Vegas, to a house run by the Franciscans, known informally as the Center for Peace (and at times also as the Bartlett Avenue Community). The purpose of this move was to put her near the Nevada Desert Experience (NDE), a group of anti-nuclear peace activists who took newcomers on an eye-opening immersion tour of US nuclear test sites, and also near the Las Vegas Catholic Worker and a related group called the Pace e Bene Nonviolence Service.

Sacred Peace Walk

She had been to NDE headquarters many times, making visits going back to the 1980s. Sometimes accompanied by her now-widowed mother Madeleine, she had participated in events such as the Sacred Peace Walk, a four-day, fifty-five-mile Holy Week pilgrimage. Guided by Chief Johnnie Bobb, a Western Shoshone spiritual person and Chief of its National Council, the walk proceeds from the Las Vegas Atomic Testing Museum in the Las Vegas suburb of Paradise, Nevada, to the Nevada National Security Site (NNSS) northwest of the city, where hundreds of above- and below-ground nuclear tests were conducted from the 1950s through the 1990s. Along the way, the pilgrims stop to pray and protest at Creech Air Force Base, from which technicians remotely engage in drone warfare in Middle Eastern nations. Chief Bobb leads sunrise ceremonies at the group's peace camp. After the Nuclear Stations of the Cross on Good Friday, groups often march on Easter Sunday across the property line at the NNSS. They trespass as an act of civil resistance, and sometimes are arrested as a result.

An NDE Sacred Peace Walk often includes drummers, dancers with white death masks similar to those used in Kabuki, and people carrying large signs with messages like "STOP KILLER DRONES," "TRY TESTING PEACE," and "THE MOST BOMBED PLACE ON EARTH." Protestors in death's-head masks have floated large, inflatable drones with the word *KILLER* on the side.

In Rice's 2013 court testimony, she described the Sacred Peace Walk experience, saying,

> We heard from the spiritual leader of the Western Shoshone people, Mr. Corbin Harney, every time. He was able to express the faith that these people who had been inhabiting this land for tens of thousands of years, what they had learned not only from the beauty that they saw, but the actual vibration, the harmonious vibrations which mountains and all things are constantly doing to give us energy and life.

> We all receive the waves from the vibrations of the moun-
> tains and the crystals and the earth, and they saw the sky,
> the air, and the sun and the water and the fire as that which
> were elements for the creation of the life of all of us.[1]

In the act of stepping across the NNSS property line, demonstrators approach slowly and respectfully, often marching
to Native drum music and following someone carrying a
cross. One by one they step over the line. They bow or kneel
down on the ground, sometimes make the sign of the cross,
and wait to be arrested. Some put out their arms to each
side in the shape of a cross, and the military police officers
dutifully step up and lift each protester by the outstretched
arms to carry/drag them away. Often the mood is hushed
and whispering, almost silent, with the brisk desert wind
whipping by. After a brief detention in permanent holding
pens set up for this purpose, the police charge the activists
with trespass, process them, and release them on-site.

Chief Johnnie Bobb developed as a spiritual person in
part by observing his grandmother, who was also one. Much
of his adult formation came from the teachings of the late
Corbin Harney, a famed elder and spiritual leader who
taught him the Western Shoshone principles of governance.
His strongest opposition to the NNSS developed after a trip
to Kazakhstan in the 1980s, visiting victims of radiation
poisoning.

Chief Bobb began an annual two-week event called the
Western Shoshone Nation's Annual Walk/Run in the late
1990s. It brings more people, including many non-Natives,
to the region to do spiritual work, learning about the land
and aligning with the Nation's goals. His partner Mary Lou
Anderson points out that because Shoshone land is the most
bombed place on the planet, the cause unites many different
groups. He explains:

I always tell the kids and the non-Natives that we are doing this [walk/run] because of the elders. They made trails in the mountains, so we have to keep our traditional gatherings and other things to keep our young ones safe, healthy, and use that water in a good way with our ceremonies.

I was the first-born, and I had a connection with the mother earth. I had connections with what I see, with what I smell and feel. I have connections with our animals out there, and I had connections with water, with springs, the rivers.

You see things out there, continuing on that journey with that vision, and the vision takes you back to understand this Nevada test site. Our animals, turtles, and everything else in that area—all are endangered species. Water is very sacred, very powerful, water can penetrate through rocks, soil. Water is something that is life to all the living things.

Corbin would always say, "We're going to stay strong, keep doing what we're doing, we have to keep on moving." How will radiation from the bombing or any other chemicals that they're using affect the people? What's going to happen to our air? Our air's going to get more polluted. Corbin would always say, "Why can't they stop making it?" Nevada is our home. Nevada is where we live. We always lived here just like any other Native people.

For me as a spiritual person, I've been raised with my [Native] language, how to use it and say where we came from. With prayer we add that our water, air, fire, and mother earth is one. I myself learned from my elders to see that we use this water for ourselves, and then other people use water for themselves, and it goes all the way around the world. We're all one people.[2]

At some of the protests, activists wail in sorrow, a lament for what the US has done to Native land. John Amidon, who developed a specific wailing protest with Candace Ross, describes to experience as "flat-out full and completely intense . . . sad/painful and cathartic, all of the three and physically exhausting." A former Marine, Amidon considers the wailing an expression of pain, "both physical and emotional. Physically to the throat, and pressure in the head. It is emotionally painful also, a true expression of grief on my part and confession. A cathartic release of some of my transgressions."[3]

The Western Shoshone people say that the activists have a legal right to cross the property line at the NNSS. They are a sovereign nation and insist that the United States government therefore has only limited rights to use their land via the 1863 Treaty of Ruby Valley. However, the government has long acted as though the treaty meant the land was surrendered for a modest payment. There is considerable debate, and although most legal opinions side with the Western Shoshone, the government isn't budging.[4]

Prior to each protest at the NNSS, Western Shoshone officials issue permits to the activists. They believe the trespass charge from the US government is actually illegal. Protesters then cross the line, holding their Western Shoshone permits, and the Nye County Sheriff's Department issues trespassing citations but does not try to enforce them. This is more than just protest theater, but an important re-assertion of legal rights on behalf of the Western Shoshone. Crossing becomes an act of civil resistance, not disobedience, as citizens accuse the government of what they believe is criminal wrongdoing.

In 2019 the Western Shoshone people issued a *Peoples' Indictment* against the US President and federal government with "crimes against peace" and "crimes against humanity" for secretly shipping Cold-War-era, weapons-grade plutonium to the NNSS. When Rice invoked the Western Shoshone people in her court testimony, she was reminding the United States that not only were nuclear weapons illegal under international law, but the US was in violation of the rights of the Western Shoshone Nation by developing and testing nuclear weapons and other systems on their land, including drones.

Kindred Spirits

Rice volunteered by repeatedly driving a van two-hundred fifty miles roundtrip to pick up and return people who had been detained for various anti-nuclear actions. She and her mother were occasionally among groups arrested at the Nevada site, and Madeleine Rice considered their time in the Nevada desert her happiest during her long struggle of living as a widow. After her mother died in 1999, Rice felt they remained together very much in spirit, including times in the desert when she felt Madeleine's presence quite vividly.

During Rice's many years living in Africa, the United States had not been anywhere near the center of her attention. Now common attitudes expressed casually in daily papers and on the news seemed imperialist to her. Most people in the United States didn't understand these perceptions. Sometimes she felt isolated, like a beloved but distrusted eccentric, babbling on about political realities of which they knew nothing. Among the Catholic Workers in Las Vegas, she found common ground. She now settled in among kindred spirits in a place that enveloped her in warmth and sunshine; she was no longer an anonymous face walking on a crowded sidewalk in between tall buildings, waiting to catch a glimpse of the sky.

Rice joined a Las Vegas Catholic Worker group about a mile from the former Franciscan friary nicknamed Bartlett for its avenue. Lay and religious activists all shared the compound. She lived in a single-story, boxy, flat-roofed building, one of several painted purple, blue, and white. Ryan Hall, the executive director of the nonprofit Pace e Bene Nonviolence Service, recalls sharing meals with Rice at Bartlett. "I always appreciated her unique take on the world. I remember telling her at one point that I was having difficulty with the Catholic Church, but she always reminded me that 'we the people are the church.' "[5]

Among the Las Vegas Catholic Workers were a Franciscan priest, Fr. Louis Vitale, and Anne Symens-Bucher, both among the group that had founded the NDE in 1983, along with a Mennonite pastor, Peter Ediger. Some of these long-time peace activists had been arrested hundreds of times. Although Rice had known them for years, this was the first time she had lived among them, and she settled right in during this new phase of her life as though it had been part of the grand plan all along.

Vitale is highly recognizable with his gray goatee and brown Franciscan habit, sporting buttons and badges with messages like "Stop Torture Now" and "Just Say No to More Money for War" in bright red. He is a combat veteran, like many others who actively supported Plowshares and Veterans For Peace. He joined ROTC in college and later was an Air Force interceptor, but he became disillusioned by the inhumanity and illogic of his combat experience during the Korean War. He said in a 2007 interview,

> We were sent up to shoot down a positively-identified Russian bomber coming into the United States, the Detroit-Chicago area. Over some hours they observed it, and they kept getting us ready on closer alert, and they . . . scrambled us to go after it.
>
> And we said, "Will we do what we call an identification pass, where you come alongside and look at it? Or do we do a ninety-degree firing pass, where you shoot it down?"

They said, "Absolutely, firing pass."
We said, "Don't you think we should look first?"
"No, it's positively identified. Firing pass."
[After] the two or three times they said that, we still went
and looked . . . and it was an airliner.[6]

In an interview with Rosalie Riegle, Vitale added, "We saw
ladies looking out the window at us."[7] Disgusted with these
realities of war versus what he imagined as an idealistic
young recruit, he became a priest and full-time peace activist in a pattern quite similar to that of Phil Berrigan. Recognizing a "deep, deep yearning inside of us for peace,"
Vitale dedicated his life to it.[8] He remembered,

> I think the first time I was arrested was in the early '70s.
> Las Vegas. We did a sit-in with welfare rights mothers on
> the Strip. I remember thinking that would be the end of
> everything in the priesthood. But it wasn't: I ended up a
> Minister to the Province, and moved to Oakland and got
> involved in Berkeley.
>
> Dan Berrigan came and got everybody all excited and
> on Ash Wednesday, probably in 1980, we sat in at the
> Chancellor's office. I remember a young friar was with us.
> He's going, "Oh my God! I'll be thrown out of the order."
>
> I said, "Don't worry. I'm the guy who would throw you
> out." So.[9]

Rice befriended another Franciscan, Fr. Jerry Zawada,
who had always been a pacifist. He was arrested for trespassing multiple times in the late 1980s, when he protested
at missile silos in the Midwest. Zawada served quite a bit
of prison time over the years, for example, after one of his
many protests of torture training at Fort Huachuca, Arizona.
In 2014, when speaking to a Franciscan novitiate group, he
laughed that one meaning of the Polish word *zawada* is

"troublemaker. . . . there's not a damned thing I can do about it. It's in my genes."[10] Zawada was notorious for a bit of protest theater that wasn't artificial at all, but sincere and close to his heart: he once celebrated Mass on the hatch of a nuclear missile. When the arresting soldiers made him lie face down on the ground, he said it gave him a "muscle memory" of his prostration before the altar at his final vows.[11]

Zawada preached practical love. Some of it came from his own backstory. He struggled as a young priest with depression and at one point took a year-and-a-half leave of absence for treatment. Although he had been living and working among the poor in the Philippines and in Chicago, all of which was in line with his values, he told a Nevada Test Site Oral History Project interviewer, "I felt like everything we were doing was Band-Aiding the problems. We had so many street people coming, people with severe mental problems and emotional problems and so on, continuously, and I felt the weight of that. I felt like I just couldn't stand it anymore and I gave up. . . . I'd never really gotten rid of this feeling of unease, and I feared working with people who were in destitute need."[12] This lasted for six or seven years, including his break, during which time he learned Spanish.

Zawada experienced a revelation during a talk at the Mexican American Cultural Center in San Antonio by Salvadoran schoolteacher Marta Alicia Rivera. She had been captured by a US-backed Salvadoran death squad and tortured in the basement of the Salvadoran National Police headquarters for thirty-two hours. Her face still bore razor scars. Her crime? Advocating for the poor, including asking for living wages, through a human-rights group the police had targeted. Upon seeing her and hearing her story, Zawada finally understood his role in the church. "I didn't have to take away anybody's pain," he said. "I just needed to walk with them and learn from them and maybe somehow. I describe it in my religious terms as seeing the face of Christ, and working along those lines just learning from them, accompanying them in their plight and then hopefully to work with others for some type of resolution and relief. But that was my indication that I needed to become political."[13]

Zawada told another interviewer how depression made it possible for him to engage meaningfully: "I could begin to walk with torture survivors. Almost every one of them comes to depression because of survival guilt. I feel close to prisoners, too, for the same reason. They have to deal with their guilt as well as with the confinement."[14]

He also returned to the priesthood understanding how to fuel himself during the journey. In that same talk to Franciscan novices, he encouraged them to see such people as "our heroes. They give us energy."[15] This reflected his new understanding, following the Rivera talk, that priests need emotional and spiritual support.

For context, we can place him in the tradition of the French worker priest movement of the mid-twentieth century. That movement attracted the US activists Daniel and Philip Berrigan because of its charism of connectedness to the lives of people. At the Casa Maria Catholic Worker in Milwaukee, Zawada said to Rosalie Riegle, "I learned that I could laugh and connect with the people living on the streets and not feel that I had to change anything. I am not God; I don't change things. I just walk with people. Accompaniment. *Acompañamiento* in Spanish. That became my sacred word."[16]

That faith-in-action focus with accompaniment as its primary method was reflected in Zawada's homilies, too. On

Easter Sunday in 2011, celebrating Mass at the entrance of the NNSS, he recounted a cartoon where a well-dressed priest entered a run-down tenement. He encouraged an overwhelmed mother caring for four tiring children by quoting St. Augustine, "Remember, woman, we are an Easter people and Alleluia is our song." It was supposed to be funny, but Zawada saw it differently after his revelation. "For God's sake, man, stop your pious rhetoric, and maybe help her, change a diaper if you need to, or at least entertain the other kids, give her a break. Or perhaps maybe even more creatively, you can find somebody from your parish that would come and help this woman. There has to be a time when we go beyond words."[17]

In 2009, he and others in the NDE joined with Kathy Kelly's Chicago-based group Voices For Creative Nonviolence in the first national gathering of prayer activists against drone violence. Rice offered a prayer during a Mass led by Zawada in the desert outside Creech Air Force Base, as the group formed a circle emanating from the altar. Rice told those gathered, "We'll just take a symbol of life, the symbol of water, and we'll pass around the water and symbolically wash our hands before we prepare for the following actions, the following days, the following weeks. [We will] enter into a deeper communion of healing and restoring the life which has been so battered on our planet."[18]

The group lived, ate, slept, and prayed at the site for a week. Occasionally they offered pizza to the guards, a specific gesture of hospitality and communion that Rice and the other Transform Now Plowshares activists would later echo at Y-12 by offering guards home-baked bread.

Zawada died in 2017, at the age of eighty. His friends and supporters held a peace vigil in his honor at Davis-Monthan Air Force Base in Tucson, Arizona.

Another of Rice's friends was former Mennonite pastor Peter Ediger, one of the cofounders of Pace e Bene Nonviolence Service who died in early 2012, just a few months before the Transform Now Plowshares Y-12 protest. Reverend Ediger's experience growing up in a Mennonite family that preached peace was interrupted by what he called the "Praise the Lord and pass the ammunition" attitudes of World War II.[19] He was drafted in 1944, but obtained conscientious objector status via his church, serving instead in an alternative program called Civilian Public Service. Mennonites did not have saints, but he read about Francis of Assisi and felt drawn to the Franciscan charism for its reverence of nature. Moving west decades later to join the group at the NDE, "this familiar brother became enfleshed," he later wrote, in the persons of Louis Vitale, Rosemary Lynch, and the others.[20] With his warm, operatic singing voice and widely-read peace-themed poetry, he became well-known in nonviolence circles.[21]

Las Vegas Catholic Worker cofounder Julia Occhiogrosso remembers Ediger coming to their community initially as part of the Lenten Desert Experience, forty days of prayer and protest outside the gate of the Nevada Test Site. He wore traditional Mennonite garb, but the longer he lived there he gradually adapted his style. He began referring to himself as a "Mennonite Franciscan," hearkening back to those early encounters with St. Francis of Assisi while doing his alternate military service.[22] There are photos of him holding signs such as "ENDING WAR: OUR Collective Responsibility" and "JESUS SAYS LOVE YOUR ENEMIES. WHAT DOES YOUR CHURCH SAY?"

These people and others became Rice's spiritual companions as she learned in the desert how to reimagine her life post-Africa.

SOA Watch

Like many activists, Rice also protested at the School of the Americas (SOA, now known as the Western Hemisphere Institute for Security Cooperation [WHINSEC]), a US Army training ground for Latin American soldiers and officers in Fort Benning, Georgia. The purpose of the program was to provide training to Latin American military personnel on US-bought artillery and weapons and in nation-building principles and strategies. Protestors accused graduates of the SOA of committing human rights violations via psychological warfare and torture that critics claimed they learned to perpetrate at the school itself. The strongest allegations said the program trained assassins and dictators, and taught soldiers how to take part in death squads. As Congressman John Lewis asked during a Congressional hearing, viewable in a fiery clip from a 1995 Maryknoll film, *School of Assassins*, "Why should we continue to train thugs to kill their own people?"[23]

In 1980, Archbishop of San Salvador Óscar Romero was shot to death while celebrating Mass. Declassified information years later showed that his killers had trained at the SOA and that they had targeted him for questioning the SOA's role in El Salvador. On November 16, 1989, the same forces slaughtered six Jesuit priests and their housekeeper in San Salvador. Nineteen of the twenty-six officers implicated were graduates of the SOA.[24]

Although Congress held hearings throughout the 1990s and reduced the SOA's allocations, they never completely defunded it. After closing for a few weeks, the program was renamed the Western Hemisphere Institute for Security Cooperation (WHINSEC) in 2001. Some courses on human rights were added, but longtime activists say it is the same old school but now with Congressional deniability. The protests continue, implicating US military intervention in Latin America as one of the root causes of the migration crisis.

Former Maryknoll priest Roy Bourgeois founded the organization SOA Watch in 1990 to draw attention to and denounce the program's practices. He imbued the organization with the spirit of his mantra, "We Are Not Made For War," a phrase in harmony with Louis Vitale's conclusion that humans have a deep yearning inside of us for peace.[25] Like several other figures in this book, Bourgeois was a veteran, a Naval officer with the red-state politics common in his Louisiana hometown of 3,500 people. He entered the military to fight Communism, but his encounters with orphans in Vietnam led him to question US military actions, particularly the use of napalm on children. He received the Purple Heart for injuries sustained in a bombing. Instead of continuing a planned career in the military, he declared the poor his teachers, and in 1966 he decided to become a missionary instead.

While studying to become a Maryknoll priest, Bourgeois refused to attend a lecture by Fr. Dan Berrigan, questioning how a man who had not served could criticize the military. While he was missioned in a poor community in Bolivia, however, Bourgeois observed US forces supporting the Banzer regime, which he knew to be a dictatorship. Later he returned to Vietnam and was sickened by how the military treated injured orphans as collateral damage instead of taking responsibility for the children's wounds that the US had inflicted.

Gradually, Bourgeois reckoned with a cumulative emotional toll as he considered how the torture and murder of his Jesuit friend Luís Espinal Camps on March 21, 1980;

the assassination of Archbishop Óscar Romero; the rape and murder of two of his personal friends, Maryknoll sisters Maura Clark and Ita Ford, with Ursuline Sr. Dorothy Kazel and laywoman Jean Donovan, in El Salvador on December 2, 1980; and the murder of six Jesuits and two laywomen in El Salvador on November 16, 1989. He tied all of these crimes back to the SOA.

On Pentecost Sunday, May 25, 1980, Baltimore's Jonah House held a Pentagon vigil. The next chapter will detail its founding contribution to Plowshares. This was a standard protest—anti-nuclear and anti-arms-race—but it took on deeper meaning for Bourgeois in light of Romero's assassination. He traveled to DC from the Catholic Worker house where he was living in Chicago and marched, holding a poster of Romero. At a Mass on the Pentagon lawn, the group prayed for America to beat its swords into plowshares. Some marchers held signs quoting Pope Paul VI, "The arms race is an intolerable scandal." The next day, May 26, Bourgeois went to the Navy office in the Pentagon and returned his Purple Heart, along with a letter of explanation.[26] In the parlance of some in Plowshares, he had "learned to see." Bourgeois also rethought his opinion of Dan and Phil Berrigan, whom he had previously dismissed. Soon he would join them in the same causes and get to know them well.

SOA Watch protests have included some annual marches around November 16, the date of 1980 murders in El Salvador. Supporters join a procession with white crosses and peace signs bearing the names of the disappeared, the tortured, and the assassinated. Black-dressed mourners with white masks carry coffins, sometimes staging die-ins. Members of the Christian Peacemaker Teams symbolically wash the US flag of its sins. They have also included the presence of large and elaborate puppets marching on stilts, three times as tall as a person and at times requiring several "pup-petistas" to operate. Chants ring out: "We'll never be di-vided, the people united" and "The walls that they built to tear us apart will never be as strong as the walls of our hearts." A professional Musicians Collective sometimes of-fers both original music and classic protest songs. And a modified litany of saints is intoned, with the crowd respond-ing in song after each name, "¡*Pre-sen-te!*"

Rice got to know many of the participants, including Ursuline Sr. Clare O'Mara, who was arrested at SOA protests in 1994 at age seventy-four. Murdered Ursuline Sr. Dorothy Kazel had been one of the latter's congregation sisters, making her brutal death quite personal. When the judge offered to let Sr. O'Mara and another woman off with probation, since there were only two women in the larger arrested group, they asked for the same prison time as their male counterparts. The judge gave them two months. In 2012 O'Mara received the "Sr. Dorothy Kazel Alleluia Award, bestowed by the Ursuline sisters of Cleveland upon a person who reflects Kazel's courage, faith, and optimism."

PLOWSHARES SACRAMENTS: BLOOD IN BABY BOTTLES

The actual pouring of the blood in a Plowshares action is an inherently mindful sacrament. Regarding its use, activ-ist Art Laffin notes, "It's a statement that we're prepared to give our life rather than take life. We want to prevent the shedding of innocent blood."[27] *Baby bottles make that innocence visual, as Boertje-Obed said at trial. "The reason we chose baby bottles, to represent that the blood of chil-dren is spilled by these weapons and in the making of these weapons and the testing of them."*[28]

The Baltimore Four used blood in their 1967 draft board action, one that would later become an integral part of the Plowshares witness. The late activist and artist Tom Lewis told Rosalie Riegle that it was Phil Berrigan's idea and that blood dripping from draft files meant the bloody death of young people in Vietnam, "a Biblical symbol and a healing symbol."[29] At the 2012 Y-12 protest, Transform Now Plowshares threw some of Lewis's banked blood on the facility's walls.

To get blood onto a huge building, wall, or vessel so that it can be seen and make enough of what journalist Rachel Maddow called, when reporting on the Y-12 action, a "peaceful mess" to be effective, it must be thrown with vigor.

Activist Lynn Fredriksson said, "We poured our own blood on one bomber to expose the bloody warmaking of the entire US military."[30] Fr. Carl Kabat didn't use blood but rather red paint when he dressed up as a clown to do his actions. Some protesters create a palm print with blood or draw a cross. Others pour it, reverently, over a bomber part or on the ground.

On All Souls Day 2009, Susan Crane, one of the five members of the Disarm Now Plowshares, carried a message with her deep into the secure bunker area of the Bangor Trident Base outside Seattle where the nuclear warheads are stored. Her message read, in part,

> We bring our own blood to pour on the missiles, nuclear weapons, trident subs, or perhaps on the railroad tracks that carry the weapons. We pour our blood to remind us all of the consequences of warmaking. We bring hammers to enflesh the words of Isaiah to hammer swords into plowshares. We bring sunflower seeds to sow to begin to convert the base, and we bring disarmed hearts in hope of a disarmed world.[31]

At the 2019 trial of the Kings Bay Plowshares 7, activist Patrick O'Neill testified, "We came to reveal what goes on there that nobody wants to go into—what weapons are and what they did. . . . The symbol of blood is a little hard to understand. But in the context of faith . . . there are two simple components. One, the sacrifice of Jesus for our sins. And then there is the blood that is the everlasting covenant. It's also what happens in war. Kings Bay is nice and clean and you never see the blood. But the plans for war go on there. So we made it more visible."[32]

Nuclear resister Frances Crowe, who died in 2019 at the age of one hundred, remembered being assaulted by a crowd after she attended the launch of a Trident submarine in Groton, Connecticut, and mocked the tradition of christening with champagne. Instead, she used a small bottle of her own blood. "The crowd surrounded me as people tore at my clothes, scratched my face and arms, and pulled my hair. I was never so relieved as when the police came to arrest me."[33]

CHAPTER THREE

Jonah House Led to Plowshares

Greg Boertje-Obed, Michael Walli, and Sr. Megan Rice have all lived at Jonah House at different times.[1] This Baltimore faith community was founded in 1973 by Elizabeth McAlister, Phil Berrigan, John Bach, Sr. Judith LaFemina, and Fr. James La Croce, after a year of meetings and discernment, a process that typifies Plowshares. Ever since Phil Berrigan, the Josephite, appeared with his brother Daniel, the Jesuit, in their clerical collars on the cover of *Time* magazine in 1971, looking more like Jimmy Cagney's gangster character than Pat O'Brien's priest in *Angels with Dirty Faces*, they had been controversial rebel icons both within their congregations and in the world at large. Phil Berrigan and Liz McAlister left their respective religious congregations to marry, but in many ways they retained their deep formations. The goal was to feed the hungry and preach peace, and it remains effective in the nuclear resistance, central to the mission of Plowshares.

The Long Stone Gaze

After getting off Interstate 95 in Baltimore and passing the Inner Harbor and Orioles Stadium, you enter Bridgeview-

Greenlawn, with nary a lawn, just treeless streets and stark row houses. People sometimes approach cars at stoplights to beg. Then you hang a left, passing the chain-link fence of a tire-recycling company, find the double mailbox, and suddenly the scene changes from bleak city to lush oasis. Jonah House sits on the property of St. Peter's Cemetery, and the diocese lets it remain there in exchange for tending the grounds. You might feel you've gone back a century when the circa-1890s stone statue of Catherine O'Grady gazes past you from the prow of her funereal ship. Next to a nearby fig tree, also in white stone, an angel interrupts a child at play, gently steering her shoulders from this life toward paradise. Under a pine near the house stands Phil Berrigan's monument, a sturdy Celtic cross that reads "LOVE ONE ANOTHER." Elmer Maas, who participated in the very first Plowshares action as one of the "Plowshares Eight" in 1980, has a marker nearby designed by an artist in the community.

There used to be goats in the cemetery and llamas to guard the goats from attack by foxes and wild dogs, but running a working farm with activists coming and going was too much work. The website archive includes many animal photographs, including one of Sr. Anne Montgomery, RSCJ, riding a donkey named Vinnie. Now the animals are just lively memories.

Thirty or so friends came together in 1995 for an old-fashioned barn raising to build the current house, replacing the first location, a rowhouse in Baltimore's Reservoir Hill neighborhood. It is spaciously comfortable, with picture windows, a long dining room table that looks handmade, and abundant plants enjoying plentiful light. The basement that opens to the outdoors has always been a food pantry, serving scores of people each week, some who beg at the cars waiting at stoplights. When the COVID crisis began in 2020, Jonah House partnered with Tubman House in the Sandtown-Winchester neighborhood to care for more people.

Jonah House is connected in spirit and history to nearby Viva House, founded and run by Brendan Walsh and Willa Bickham. Walsh was Daniel Berrigan's theology student at Le Moyne College in 1962–63. He became a member of the International House that Berrigan founded. He and Bickham met Dan's brother Phil in 1967 and worked with him for thirty-five years. They knew David Miller—credited with being the very first American to burn his draft card for Vietnam, for which he was sentenced to Lewisburg Penitentiary—as Miller and his wife Catherine were both Le Moyne graduates and close friends of Daniel. Walsh and Bickham became part of the support committee for the Catonsville Nine, and Walsh was one of the drivers who took the Berrigan brothers to the Catonsville draft board in May 1968.[2]

The couple founded Viva House shortly thereafter as, in part, a place for hospitality to activists. Many draft resisters lived with them, including Tom Lewis and John Hogan of the Catonsville Nine and Jim Harney of the Milwaukee Fourteen. The FBI often watched the house and questioned the neighbors. Today Viva House is so iconic that in 2007 it was even featured in an episode of the acclaimed HBO series *The Wire*, with the couple playing themselves.[3] McAlister and Berrigan helped Bickham and Walsh begin and grow Viva House as part of the Baltimore Catholic Worker community. Bickham in turn helped Berrigan and McAlister find the original Jonah House site.

> *There are many homes in Baltimore that have a careful coat of paint put on by some of the most famous jailbirds in America.*
>
> Garry Wills[4]

Jonah House is named for the prophet who served his time in the belly of a whale, and the name also reminds some people of the leviathan of the US penal corrections system. John Bach says that there was an actual little ivory statue of Jonah that the early founders liked, so they used the name when setting up the house's first checking account.[5] Author Jim Forest, a longtime friend and collaborator of the Berrigans, considers the name appropriate, since Jonah tried to warn and save Nineveh just as the activists in the house want to warn and save America.[6] The founders designed Jonah House as a place where activists could be known, understood, and—in their characteristically edgy way—nurtured. Although most priests and sisters make annual retreats to refresh the spirit, it was not always possible for Plowshares activists and other Catholic Workers to find retreat directors who could understand and appreciate their unique and exhausting work. Many church leaders disapproved of it. So Jonah House became a designated stopover. It held training sessions on civil resistance, teaching its members how to take direct political action together, including how to do a "die-in" at the Pentagon, how to get arrested (everything from what to wear to how much money to bring to bail yourself out), and how to run discernment weekends that are the usual run-up to a full-blown Plowshares action.[7]

Sr. Carol Gilbert, OP, explains that most Catholic Workers prefer the term *civil resistance* to *civil disobedience*, because the former describes activity that is legal, the latter illegal. They avoid strictly illegal actions on principle, as their purpose is not to break the law but to call us to a higher law. Gilbert said that resisters remind the world of the Nuremberg principles defining what constitutes a war crime: (1) crimes against peace, (2) crimes against humanity, (3) violations of the laws of war, and (4) conspiracies to commit the first three criminal acts. Occasionally, albeit rarely, judges agree.[8] International human rights lawyer Francis Boyle compares civil resisters to law enforcement, with a duty to hold our government accountable to its own Constitution and to its treaties with Native Americans and others. "Today's civil resisters are the sheriffs," he wrote around the time of the troop surge during the Iraq war in 2007. "The Bush Administration officials are the outlaws."[9]

> *"Resister" has a double meaning when you look at it carefully: Re-sister.*
> *Art Laffin, Dorothy Day Catholic Worker*[10]

Unlike retreat houses where sacred texts and religious books were the only reading and conversation fare, at Jonah House it was also normal to add multiple newspapers each day, while engaging in near-constant social analysis. The Pacifica news organization's radio program *Democracy Now!*—where most of the house's residents have been featured over the years—became a soundtrack. "Everybody knew the routine of Jonah House," recalls Mary Novak. "We're up at six, prayer at seven, and we're listening to Amy Goodman at eight."[11] Books such as Howard Zinn's *A People's History of the United States* and William Stringfellow's *An Ethic for Christians and Other Aliens in a Strange Land* and *My People Is the Enemy* became essential in the early years. This admiration for left-leaning intellectuals was mutual, with Zinn speaking at his friend Philip Berrigan's funeral, while Goodman recorded it for *Democracy Now!*

The community had only one television, hidden out of sight. Early members perceived quotidian broadcasts as both inaccurate and mind-numbing, although that position has softened somewhat. In lieu of TV in the evenings, guests such as Anne Montgomery who had "rolled in" (an early Jonah House term for coming off the road for a respite) would join the gathered circle after dinner and share quite literal war stories from her travels in the combat zones of Afghanistan and Iraq, or her exploits being arrested for anti-nuclear activities.

Jonah House differs from Catholic Worker communities in how it functions in the world. Members needed the flexibility to go places freely, whether to the picket line or to prison, so the house couldn't serve the poor the same way Catholic Worker houses did. Instead, the community painted houses so that when something came up, such as an impending Plowshares action, they would be free to act. However, this could lead to misunderstandings. In some media profiles, for example, Michael Walli was identified as a "house painter," but it is rarely noted that *all* of the Jonah House residents from a certain cohort painted houses. They chose the work because it went quickly and paid in cash, which enabled Jonah House members to stick to their ethos of not paying taxes to fund government violence in all its forms. Dull, repetitive painting could also become a form of prayer. As John Dear recalls in his 1995 incarceration memoir, *Peace Behind Bars: A Peacemaking Priest's Journal from Jail*, "When [Phil Berrigan] and Liz McAlister are painting houses (to earn a living), Phil takes hours to contemplate the Lord's prayer and the Magnificat. Liz does the same: no formal prayer time, no long wordy prayers—just a life of contemplative prayer."[12]

Greg Boertje-Obed said, "[Y]our schedule was flexible. You could go to demonstrations, you could go to jail. There were enough people that the painting could continue with a few people away. Now they mow lawns."[13]

In fact, knowledge of painting became an asset during the trial for Transform Now Plowshares. Boertje-Obed challenged the government's assertion that the cost of cleanup was over $7,500 after their action by questioning the need for one hundred gallons of paint for one defaced wall. He estimated one gallon would have been plenty.[14]

So far the description isn't that much different from other notable intentional communities, such as Viva House, Twin Oaks in Louisa, Virginia—the oldest continually-running commune in the United States, long-known for nonviolence and political action—or Fr. Edward Guinan's Community for Creative Nonviolence (CCNV) in Washington, DC, which famously advocated for the homeless in the 1980s. CCNV activist Mitch Snyder met the Berrigans and John Bach while in Danbury Prison, joined their book group, and embraced their radical Gospel. Although he became the most famous face of CCNV before his 1990 suicide, it was the day-to-day commitment of the Paulist priest Guinan, who founded it, and the visionary leadership of Ed and Kathleen Guinan together after he left the Paulists, that built it into a city icon. These groups lived simply and cheaply as part of their radical solidarity with the working poor.

What made Jonah House special was a particular kind of activist formation that occurred within each participant. As Paul Magno, a Georgetown University alumnus who has lived at Jonah House at various times and who traveled with Megan Rice throughout Europe after her release to share the message, explains, "Jonah House became a graduate school of nonviolent resistance that has incubated scores of individuals, communities, and movements. They have the wherewithal to do this kind of work for decades, rooted in faith and in critical analysis of the world we live in. [People learn to see] through the 'BS,' as Phil might have seen it, and speak and, more importantly, act sacrificially [with] the humane possibilities God made us for."[15]

Rice lived at Jonah House off and on before and after she left Nigeria. Life in the Jonah House community could take a physical and mental toll, but she felt up to it. Decades of harder living in Africa left her exceptionally well prepared for early mornings and physically demanding actions. Rice met Phil Berrigan at Jonah House and felt great respect for his work, but from a cultural and emotional distance after so many years living abroad. She felt most connected when they did outdoor things with the group, like chopping wood.

To understand why she needed the Berrigan influence to become an activist, and then why she needed to leave, it helps to know more about Phil, who sometimes got lost in the shadow of his more mediagenic brother Dan, but who, in Plowshares and Jonah House contexts, has an interesting central role.

> "Him again," he shouted, pointing one large fist at [Phil Berrigan's] head. "Good God, I'm changing my religion."
>
> A Catholic FBI agent at the arrest of the Catonsville Nine[16]

Berrigan's Skirmishes with Empire

The legacy of Josephite Phil Berrigan and his Jesuit brother Daniel is essential to understanding the origins of Plowshares. Although they are both foundational, they can also run away with the story, and one key point of this book is that Plowshares isn't the work of a few stars, but of many committed people working at a grassroots level. Therefore we'll consider Phil Berrigan's life but then move him off the stage, since so many other activists have played such vital roles. Much of what follows is drawn from his 1996 memoir, *Fighting the Lamb's War: Skirmishes with the American Empire.*

After a tough childhood in a home that was both loving and violent, Phil Berrigan's formation—odd in the story of a life rooted in peace, but typical in Plowshares—truly started in the Army. He was a combat soldier in World War II's Battle of the Bulge alongside his older brother Tom. While their more literary brother Dan, who had physical limitations, entered the Jesuits and became a noted poet, Phil Berrigan was eager to fight what he perceived as a just war. Religious and also trusting his country's stated reasons for entering the war, he wanted to "join the hunt for Adolf Hitler, to hack him into pieces, and to count the demons as they flew out of his wounds."[17] He also wanted to punch his father back somehow.

By his own account he became a "highly skilled young killer," capable with a bayonet and a submachine gun. He witnessed atrocities, such as the time he and a buddy stumbled into a subbasement stacked with bodies in bombed-out Muenster, Germany, where Nazi doctors had performed experiments on corpses. While getting slugged by a father who also loves you while growing up, and then being trained to kill people in a war you learn to loathe, is not a typical background for a future pacifist, it placed him beyond any criticism that peaceniks are either weaklings or unpatriotic. It also made him ready-to-die brave, which is part of why Plowshares has such an edge.

After graduating from the College of the Holy Cross on the GI Bill, he joined the Society of St. Joseph of the Sacred Heart (known as Josephites), a religious community of Catholic priests and brothers known for its charism toward and with people of color. Berrigan chose this direction out of his disgust over the blatant, relentless racism he witnessed in the military toward African-Americans who fought the war. While Megan Rice was finishing her master's degree in the 1950s, Phil Berrigan was ministering in DC's historically Black Anacostia neighborhood. When she left for Nigeria in 1962, he was serving a seven-year stint of ministry in a Black New Orleans parish. He eventually came to understand the priesthood as part of the power structure and hence compromised. Connecting racism, poverty, and militarism (taxing the poor to build bombs rather than schools), he began to write. His long pieces in *The Priest* magazine and *The Catholic Worker* newspaper about racial issues in the South made white Christians uncomfortable and brought the censure of his superiors.

Meanwhile his Jesuit brother Dan published his first book of poetry, winning the Lamont Poetry Prize and eventually, after more publications and growing prominence, being nominated for a National Book Award. The Berrigans combined their budding fame with a mutual sense that the priesthood meant more than reinforcing the prejudices of the white, suburban nuclear family and supporting the war-strong US status quo. Emulating French "worker priests" they met in Europe, who walked with their people on the picket lines and hauled nets with fishermen, the Berrigans gradually stepped into meatier roles.

In 1964, when Rice had been in Nigeria for two years and sensed the tensions that would lead that country to civil war and famine, Phil and Dan Berrigan were publicly protesting the Vietnam War in Lafayette Park, across from the White House, with Joan Baez, Rabbi Abraham Feinberg, A. J. Muste, David Dellinger, and many other famous activists. They were all over the papers in the United States, but Rice never heard of them and would not until she returned to New York on her first home leave.

On October 17, 1967, Phil Berrigan and three other demonstrators—the press dubbed them the Baltimore Four—carried out a dramatic public protest. Phil Berrigan wrote, "Tom Lewis, David Eberhardt, Jim Mengel, and I did walk into the Baltimore Customs House. We did attempt to destroy draft records, pouring our own blood over licenses to kill human beings. . . . Vietnam was burning. Watts, Newark, Detroit were burning."[18] Eberhardt, a poet and musician from a prep school background, went to Oberlin and then dropped out of the Peace Corps. He returned to Baltimore and felt bored teaching at Boys Latin Prep while trying to become "a real person." Participation in the Baltimore Four animated him, and his only regret is not joining the subsequent Catonsville Nine. He eloquently describes how the preparation of three institutions—prep school, college, and prison—gave his life meaning, and after serving twenty-one months he worked for twenty years within the system, devoting himself to Offender Aid and Restoration, "one of the few ex-convicts who actually found a career because of my prison experience."[19] He joins many others in framing his prison experience as essential formation for a life of resistance and contemplation.

The Baltimore Four inspired a better-known action that caught Rice's attention. The protest by the Catonsville Nine on May 17, 1968, essentially became the mother of Plowshares. Phil Berrigan had not even been sentenced yet for the Baltimore Four action when he engaged in yet another shocking protest: "On May 17, 1968, eight friends and I struck again, this time at a draft board in Catonsville, Maryland, where we carried hundreds of draft records into the parking lot and doused them with homemade napalm. . . . We watched the records burn, we prayed, and waited to be arrested."[20]

The homemade napalm was a protest against the US military's use of napalm on civilians in Vietnam. Some say Catholic Worker Tom Lewis found the recipe—gasoline and laundry soap—in Georgetown University's law library. Others have credited it to Jesuit Richard McSorley locating it there, specifically in a Special Forces handbook, but in his autobiography *My Path to Peace and Justice*, McSorley does not take credit for it. Fr. McSorley, who comes into this story later, had been invited to join the group but did not, a decision he attributes to being too concerned about saving his "own sweet skin," using Dan Berrigan's words about himself, and one that he, like Dave Eberhardt, later regretted.[21] McSorley was a passionate Catholic Worker who had marched with Martin Luther King Jr., in Selma and who perpetually agitated publicly against ROTC on Georgetown's main campus. His picture hangs today at the Dorothy Day Catholic Worker house in Washington, DC, which he cofounded. He inspired many activists, including his student Paul Magno.

"A moral straight line runs from the Baltimore Four and Catonsville Nine to the Plowshares," says Magno. "These actions commenced in September 1980. Their most recent incarnation, the Kings Bay Plowshares 7—a group of seven activists, including Jonah House cofounder Liz McAlister, who entered the Kings Bay Naval Submarine Base in protest against nuclear weapons on April 4, 2018—takes place just shy of fifty years after Catonsville, on the fiftieth anniversary of Martin Luther King's martyrdom."[22]

From the Statement of the Plowshares Eight

We commit civil [resistance] at General Electric because this genocidal entity is the fifth leading producer of weaponry in the US. To maintain this position, GE drains $3 *million a day from the public treasury, an enormous larceny against the poor. We also wish to challenge the lethal lie spun by GE through its motto, "We bring good things to life." As manufacturers of the Mark 12A reentry vehicle, GE actually prepares to bring good things to death. Through the Mark 12A, the threat of first-strike nuclear war grows more imminent. Thus GE advances the possible destruction of millions of innocent lives. . . .*

In confronting GE, we choose to obey God's law of life, rather than a corporate summons to death. Our beating of swords into plowshares is a way to enflesh this biblical call. In our action, we draw on a deep-rooted faith in Christ, who changed the course of history through his willingness to suffer rather than to kill. We are filled with hope for our world and for our children as we join in this act of resistance.[23]

Actions Become Plowshares

The first Plowshares action, commonly referred to as "the Plowshares Eight," happened in 1980.[24] It was conceived in prayer and reflection by Anne Montgomery, RSCJ; Dan and Phil Berrigan; Molly Rush, a founder of the Thomas Merton center in Pittsburgh; John Schuchardt, a lawyer and Marine first lieutenant; Carl Kabat, an Oblate of Mary Immaculate missionary; Dean Hammer, a Yale Divinity graduate; and Elmer Maas, a teacher and musician.

The Brandywine Peace Community in Pennsylvania provided much of their spiritual and financial support, which is why they chose Pennsylvania. Activists in the Covenant Peace Community in New Haven, Connecticut, also supported the action and offered prayerful presence throughout the subsequent trial as well.

Eight peacemakers entered the General Electric plant in King of Prussia, Pennsylvania, chosen because the plant manufactured nose cones for Mark 12-A nuclear warheads. They beat on two of the nose cones with hammers and poured human blood on documents, in a manner reminiscent of the Baltimore Four, Catonsville Nine and other related actions such as the Camden 28, Chicago Eight, D.C. Nine, Harrisburg Seven, Milwaukee Fourteen, or Silver Spring Three. Then they waited for arrest, a method that characterized subsequent Plowshares actions. The eight were arrested, tried by a jury, convicted, and sentenced to prison terms ranging from eighteen months to ten years. After a series of appeals over a decade, they were resentenced to time served. The events were depicted in a 1983 movie, *In the King of Prussia*; the eight activists played themselves and the trial judge was played by Martin Sheen.

Phil Berrigan continued to do Plowshares actions for the rest of his life. He and his groups maintained a consistency that differentiated them from grandstanders. As he said in an interview during the period of the trial in 1981,

> What we're trying to do very, very simply is witness to life and to its sanctity out of our tradition. We are trying to say something about the truth of our times. And the fact that we hang in there over a period of maybe fifteen, sixteen, or twenty years, whatever it amounts to, that's traceable more to our tradition and to events than any sort of fixation or hysteria on our part—compulsion on our part— that's not true at all. If the warmakers would stop making the bombs and would go into disarmament, we'd go back to working with the poor, because we come from that tradition. I was serving black people in the deep South for a very, very long time before I got involved in the anti-war movement. And I'd be delighted—if peace were to arrive and disarmament happened internationally—I'd be delighted to go back to that.[25]

Dan Berrigan never took part in another Plowshares action, notes Magno, though he was a perpetual advocate for them and the people who did them. He was also a character witness for Anne Montgomery at the Pershing Plowshares trial in 1984.

Despite the inherent controversies, many chose to emulate Phil Berrigan and Liz McAlister. Daniel Sicken remembers Phil Berrigan's "walk around the block," a phrase that became well known among activists for a stroll through the neighborhood near Jonah House where Phil would convince someone to participate. They had learned the hard way not to talk on the phone with anyone, since the FBI had them tapped for years. Sicken recalled actually walking around the Jonah House block with Phil while being invited to join a Plowshares group that was starting to form.[26]

Many of the voluntary deprivations and practices of the Jonah House community—driving less, not flying in planes unless absolutely necessary, growing or foraging food rather than buying it, staying physically fit to be able to create a ruckus by climbing walls or trees to hang peace banners—prepared hardy souls like Montgomery, McAlister, Rice, Walli, Boertje-Obed, Fr. Steve Kelly, and so many others to put themselves in harm's way. All of them had developed a deep and daily prayer life, self-possession, and a willingness to be part of a mission greater than their individual needs. Whether they came from the rigors of religious life, lay life in the military, or both, further formation in this unusual and tough context became an all-purpose starting place, giving them a baseline that allowed them to take the next step and participate in more specific processes leading up to either Plowshares actions or missions with international Christian Peacemaker Teams.

Almost all young couples with children learned quickly that it made no sense for both of them to risk arrest together, for they might be incarcerated at the same time, leaving their children to be raised by others in the community. In her memoir, Frida Berrigan recalled a time in early 1977, when she was three and her brother Jerry was two, that both of her parents, Liz McAlister and Phil Berrigan, were arrested in separate actions and jailed at the same time. They hadn't anticipated this terrible accident, and it resulted in community members caring for the children full time for three months. In such a tight-knit community this worked out well enough, and the couple who stepped up to help was highly responsible, but Berrigan still recalls tears and nightmares, because it is terrifying for children so small to suddenly lose both parents. This led to a general rule that parents should orchestrate their potential arrests so that children were not left alone. Greg Boertje-Obed and his wife Michele Naar-Obed were careful not to do this to their daughter.[27]

Rice left Jonah House in 2000, explaining to her spiritual director Fr. Samson that she did not feel she was needed there any longer. Before she did, she was honored to be able to travel with Greg Boertje-Obed and five-year-old Rachel to visit Michele Naar-Obed when she was in prison for a Plowshares action, and Rice felt a growing affinity with that family. She watched Rachel while the parents visited privately, and Rice wondered about how traumatic it must be for a little girl to give up her mother for a prison term at such a young age. She remembers getting down on all fours like a horse and letting Rachel climb on her back for a ride. She and Rachel remain close, and Rice has visited Rachel's home and family in Duluth.

When Rice refers to leaving Jonah House, she sometimes shrugs and says with a wry smile that she was "fired," but it wasn't quite that contentious. It was simply time to go. She sometimes speaks of Jonah House as a specific training ground for her and then says she "graduated." Her participation in Y-12 never could have happened without it.

She returned one last time in 2002 to attend Phil Berrigan's funeral. Then she left Jonah House for what was truly the last time, carrying in her heart its deep and abiding formation.

PLOWSHARES SACRAMENTS: HAMMERS

The words of Isaiah are a powerful driving force for the Plowshares movement. Hammers remind activists that the lofty goal of this work is to abolish nuclear weapons, so that nations "shall beat their swords into plowshares, and their spears into pruning hooks; nation shall not lift up sword against nation, neither shall they learn war anymore" (2:4).

Greg Boertje-Obed explained that using a hammer to disarm a weapon can seem counterintuitive, because a hammer is so small and a nuclear weapon is so huge. Some activists don't even use full-sized work hammers, but rather the lighter type that is easier to carry. There's no way such a petite tool could truly disarm a Trident submarine the length of two football fields and capable of inflicting the damage of a hundred Hiroshima-type bombs. But the act of hammering, he said, is both a symbol and—they emphasize—an act of actual disarmament at the same time. To illustrate, he recalled hammering on an anti-submarine warplane. "Two of us hammered on a combat helicopter and a fighter bomber jet. Elmer Maas was real big on that. You render it unusable at that existential moment."[28]

Anne Montgomery said hammering was "both real and symbolic. In other words, we wanted, nonviolently and without threatening anybody, to take apart a real warhead, the Mark 12A, which we knew was being manufactured in the King of Prussia plant. And this is particularly significant because it is a first-strike weapon and because it shows the corporate connection with the Pentagon, that GE is making a lot of money, you know, millions of dollars."[29] *In a radio interview with Disarm Now Plowshares in November of 2009, she said, "We were convicted for hammering on that with hammers which represent taking something apart to turn it into something useful, like a washing machine."*

Art Laffin said, "When I was on the Trident hammering [with the 1982 Trident Nein Plowshares action], I mean, I was praying. I was praying for my own disarming of my heart, and then to say to the sailors that we encountered, and then going to court and to say to the nation and to the world: 'These weapons are immoral, they're illegal. They have no right to exist. Their only purpose is to destroy life. We are here to save life. We can disarm. We can.' "[30]

Activist Lynn Fredrikkson, who hammered in 1993 at the Seymour Johnson Air Force Base with Phil Berrigan, John Dear, and Bruce Friedrich, agreed: "We hammered on that bomber to begin the process of disassembly and conversion."[31]

The Kings Bay Plowshares 7 used special hammers for their action, made from recast guns. In this sense they used plowshares made from swords in order to hammer swords into plowshares.

Many hammers used by the activists have words on them. For the Y-12 action, Transform Now Plowshares member brought his or her own hammer. Michael Walli brought a ball-peen hammer with a cloth tied to it that bore quotations from Fr. Richard McSorley—"It is a sin to build a nuclear weapon"—and President Eisenhower—"Every dollar that is spent on armaments is a theft from the poor." Megan Rice's was a standard hammer with "Swords into plowshares, transform now into life for all" emblazoned on the handle along with the names of Western Shoshone tribe leader Corbin Harney and Rice's uncle Walter Hooke. Greg Boertje-Obed brought a small sledgehammer with "Repent! God's kindom is at hand" burned into the handle. Some Plowshares activists prefer the word kindom to kingdom, for its gesture away from a regal, masculine term, and toward the kinship of community. For her actions, Sr. Ardeth Platte's hammer bore the painted words "LOVE ENEMIES" and "DO GOOD." A hammer for the Martin Marietta MX Witness in 1985, a Plowshares-type action performed by Al Zook, Mary Sprunger-Froese, and Marie Nord, had an elaborate handle painted white with colorful words that said, "The Earth is the Lord's and the Witness Thereof," "Thou Shalt Not Kill," "LOVE your enemies and PRAY for those who persecute you," "Behold, I make all things NEW," and finally, "Jesus Wept."

Sue Frankel-Streit's hammer at the ANZUS Plowshares in 1991 said "PREPARE the WAY of the LORD." Moana Cole's at the same action said, "FAITH in JESUS is Freedom." At the HMS Vanguard Disarmament Action in Scotland in 2001, activists had a sign that showed a hammer bending a trident arrow, with the words "Tri-denting it."

Rice sometimes brings her hammer with her to events, showing it to the audience. She brought it with her to a book signing event at a Washington DC bookstore in December of 2019, which she attended as a contributor to the book, Activist: Portraits of Courage, edited by KK Ottesen. As fans gathered afterward to ask her to sign her portrait in the book, she let people who asked to do so hold the hammer. Some marveled that it was so small.[32]

CHAPTER FOUR

To Know Megan Rice, Meet Anne Montgomery

On November 2, 2009, six years after Megan Rice moved to Las Vegas, her life changed, thanks to the work of another Catholic sister. That All Souls Day, a group calling itself Disarm Now Plowshares cut through two wire fences at Naval Base Kitsap-Bangor on Puget Sound outside Seattle, Washington. The base held the largest stockpile of operational nuclear weapons in the United States. The activists splashed baby bottles of their blood on the ground and used small hammers to beat on fences and the surfaces of roadways essential to the Trident submarine system. Finally, they scattered sunflower seeds around the base.

This Plowshares action made national news. The group of five included William "Bix" Bichsel, SJ; Susan Crane; Lynne Greenwald; Steve Kelly, SJ; and Anne Montgomery, RSCJ. Their story is told in detail in a 2017 film, *The Nuns, The Priests, and The Bombs*, directed by Helen Young, which premiered at the United Nations. Young is an Emmy award-winning former CBS and NBC news producer now devoted to telling the story of Plowshares, and her work reflects their ethos accurately.

Peace in Common

Rice knew Anne Montgomery, one of the original King of Prussia Plowshares Eight in 1980, from occasional encounters at Jonah House in the late 1990s. They also had an even more personal connection going back to Rice's youth, but they didn't remember it until a bit later in their friendship. Because of Montgomery, Rice became more aware of this Washington State action, and she attended the trial in Tacoma in early 2010. Although Rice didn't realize it at the time, Montgomery would become the most significant factor in her decision to move into the work of Plowshares and eventually put herself in mortal danger.

"She was fueled by a passion for peace that was so strong," said Sr. Anne Wachter, remembering Anne Montgomery from their shared time living and ministering in East Harlem. Wachter's youth in Omaha, Nebraska, near Offutt Air Force Base, Strategic Air Command Headquarters, meant experiencing nuclear attack drills in fallout shelters long after the rest of the country ended its 1950s panic, and this made her deeply sensitive to and appreciative of Montgomery's work. "I was just really very proud of her and the way she had the courage to live her conviction . . . [She] somehow always stayed up to date on what was going on in our Society [of the Sacred Heart] . . . even when she was in prison."[1]

Almost everyone who talks about Anne Montgomery mentions her diminutive size, noting the contrast between her frail appearance and her fearless actions. Nancy Kehoe,

RSCJ, recalled, "She was so thin, [you'd think] a slight breeze would blow her away, but she had such a large passion for peace and nuclear justice issues."[2] Referring to the 1989 Thames River Plowshares action, Virginia Dennehy, RSCJ, agreed: "What touched me was that she was so tiny. And yet, she was able to swim out to the submarines."[3] Montgomery commented on that action in a 2012 interview:

> The Thames River Plowshares also stands out because of the sense of vulnerability I felt in the face of our nation's addiction to power and greed, in the face of such blasphemous power. On Labor Day 1989, we swam in freezing water for an hour and a half in the Thames River in Connecticut to reach the Trident nuclear sub, which was being readied for sea trials. Three boarded it from a canoe; those of us who were swimming got caught in the tide. Some reached the side and hammered on it.
>
> I'll never forget the vulnerability of that swim in the face of the most powerful and deadly weapon on earth. If we want to change hearts and minds, we have to come from that position of vulnerability and trust in God.[4]

All of the sisters who spoke about Montgomery emphasized how she never made anyone feel inadequate for not doing what she was doing. She lived her faith, but she didn't make her sisters feel lesser for their more traditional contributions.

Sergio Vasquez, an Associate of the Sacred Heart who was a campus minister at Convent of the Sacred Heart High School in San Francisco, remembers Montgomery as an "incredibly powerful" presence.[5] Every year, he shared with his students the story of Montgomery's July 1982 "Trident Nein" action with other Plowshares activists in Groton, Connecticut. Though nine activists were involved, they used the German word *Nein* both because of its meaning ("no") and to evoke the comparison of the Trident with the ovens of Nazi Germany.

Montgomery and eight other Plowshares activists, including her later coauthor Art Laffin, entered the Electric Boat shipyard. Four of them canoed out to the Trident, hammered and poured blood on missile hatches, and painted "USS Auschwitz" on the submarine with spray paint. This echoed the words of Seattle Archbishop Raymond Hunthausen, who had recently called the Trident "The Auschwitz of Puget Sound." Hunthausen had been strongly influenced by Jim and Shelley Douglass, whose Ground Zero Center for Nonviolent Action was directly adjacent to that naval base.

Art Laffin went with Montgomery and three others into the south storage yard. He recalls hammering with her on sonar spheres that the Navy called the eyes and ears of the Trident submarine. The five also hung a banner that said, "Trident—A Holocaust—An Oven Without Walls." This came from a line attributed to Dorothy Day about nuclear weapons: "Is there a difference between throwing innocent people into ovens and throwing ovens at innocent people?" Laffin recalled how the Trident Nein group poured their own blood at the scene, similar to the way they did it at the Disarm Now Plowshares action that drew Rice's attention.

> *Our security as people of faith lies not in demonic weapons, which threaten all life on earth. Our security is in a loving, caring God. We must dismantle our weapons of terror and place our reliance on God.*[6]
>
> *Archbishop Raymond Hunthausen*

Anne Montgomery saw herself as an ordinary person, not a hero. She considered these actions as possible even for

average citizens: "There *is* something seemingly helpless ordinary people *can* do. [They can] begin disarmament if their
leaders refuse," she wrote in a letter to a group of students
found in Sr. Megan Rice's papers. She noted that you don't
have to start with a major protest or action right away, because it comes from within: "The process includes disarming
ourselves of small violences and hateful thoughts."[7] Laffin
recalls that "Sr. Anne was a true contemplative at heart,
because you could see everything that she did was coming
from her prayer and her faith and spirituality."[8]

Christian Peacemaker Teams

In between these Plowshares actions, Montgomery engaged
in global fieldwork as a volunteer for Christian Peacemaker
Teams (CPTs). CPTs began in the 1990s to solicit invitations
from civilians in war-torn countries such as Colombia, Iraq,
Haiti, Afghanistan, and Palestine to intervene for peace. Citizens of these troubled nations collaborated with CPT, engaging together in grassroots positive resistance, prayer, and
fasting to counter violence. Montgomery once described a
CPT trip to Guantanamo Bay, Cuba, where the military
"pointed all their war energy at us," meaning showed up with
guns aimed, even though they were there to simply pray.[9]

Carolyn Osiek, RSCJ, archivist for the US-Canada Province of the Sacred Heart, describes the Israel-Palestine effort
as CPT's longest-running, most emotionally rich, and most
dangerous program; more CPT volunteers were arrested
and assaulted in Hebron than anywhere else. Osiek offers
a first-person recollection of Montgomery's work in Hebron:
"[We visited her near] the Shrine of the Patriarchs, heavily
guarded on both sides, Arab and Jewish, to keep them apart
from each other. The tension was awful. Anne explained

that their job was to monitor violations of the fragile situation. What struck me was her extraordinary courage and calmness in remaining in a place that was so volatile it could have blown up anytime."[10]

Pacifist, author, and speaker Kathy Kelly remembers being with Montgomery in Iraq in 1991 as part of the Gulf Peace Team, a group of activists who made themselves physically present in areas where military activities were expected to break out, intending to interrupt them. They collaborated to prepare for a summer peace delegation to Bosnia. Then Montgomery began what Kelly described as "extraordinary" work in Sarajevo in 1992, arranging hospitality for peace workers planning their visit while the war continued. Montgomery also visited refugees in Amman, Jordan, following the 2003 "shock and awe" bombing of Baghdad, Iraq, by the United States.[11]

Rice had spent her own time in Palestine in 1986, while on a sabbatical from her work in Nigeria, and it gave her and Montgomery a significant point of early conversation. Rice had taken a grant-funded course led by the Sisters of Notre Dame de Sion, focusing on relationships between Israelis and Palestinians. The course brought together interested Muslims, Jews, and Christians, while providing an in-person experience that Rice could draw on when teaching about the region back in Nigeria and Ghana. When she later visited Montgomery in prison, Palestine and CPT work were among the very first things they discussed.

A Daughter of the Navy

Like so many Plowshares activists, Montgomery's background included contact with the military. In her case, this came not through direct combat experience, as it did for Phil

Berrigan or Louis Vitale. Rather, she was the daughter of one of the towering figures of twentieth-century warfare, and he influenced every aspect of her life. Alfred Eugene Montgomery rose to the rank of rear admiral (temporarily vice admiral) in the Navy, with a career spent on battleships and submarines. After the bombing of Pearl Harbor on December 7, 1941, he immediately entered the action of World War II, eventually leading many of the USA's most significant sea attacks against the Japanese, including a Gilbert Islands air raid in 1943 and air raids and sea attacks around the Marshall Islands and Wake Island in 1944. "Competent, bright, and battle-tested" is the way William Trimble, former Distinguished Chair of Naval Heritage at the US Naval Academy, described him.[12] Among "Monty's" many awards were the Legion of Merit, the Distinguished Service Medal, and the Navy Cross.

It might be tempting to jump to the conclusion that Anne Montgomery's anti-war activism grew out of a troubled relationship with this celebrated but difficult man. After all, his men described him as "impatient, sarcastic, irascible except in battle, when he was calm and thoughtful, not popular, but respected."[13] He also suffered from severe migraines. What must he have been like at home? Despite these complex characterizations, however, no one who knew her well thought the "father issues" theory rang true when asked about it. Montgomery criticized all wars, but always spoke well of her father as a person. Her longtime close friend and lawyer Blake Kremer described her family as loving and supportive of each other.[14] So why did she become an adult whose actions seemed to repudiate her father's career?

The answer seems to lie more clearly in the nature of nuclear weapons themselves. Because nukes by definition targets civilians, Plowshares activists point out that they are illegal by their very existence. Use of any weapon that targets civilians is a war crime, putting nukes in the same unaccept-able category as chemical weapons and landmines, the lat-ter two of which Anne Montgomery's father would never have approved. This is part of why Plowshares activists say that their actions against nuclear weapons are legal. In a broader sense, though, many activists state that all war is criminal. But perhaps her views were even more complex. John Amidon of Veterans For Peace writes,

> The line separating military action from a war crime is an illusion. [M]urder—regardless of any legal sanction by the state under the guise of defense or war—[is] wrong, and the fiction that only combatants were targeted in an hon-orable war [is] completely dismissed as false when examin-ing military actions of any war. Nuclear weapons were particularly egregious in their offense, targeting entire cit-ies along with destroying every living creature indiscrimi-nately. Plowshares activists rightly insist nuclear weapons are illegal by their very existence. Thus none of the Plow-shares actions against nuclear weapons can be considered crimes at all. It would be a sin and a crime not to speak out against a weapon that targets life itself.[15]

Plowshares activists often cite versions of Amidon's last line as part of the "necessity defense" in court, offering it as just one of many reasons that justify trespassing at military sites and disarming nuclear weapons. If a defendant or lawyer can prove that breaking the law prevents more harm than it causes, then "the right to choose the lesser evil" (a widely accepted legal concept) should prevail.[16]

Through her family, Anne Montgomery knew the horrors of war so personally that she may further have opposed nuclear weapons on the same grounds that Louis Vitale did when he saw combat in Korea, Phil Berrigan did after he fought in World War II, or Greg Boertje-Obed, Michael Walli, and Ellen Barfield, the latter a veteran who assisted with the logistics of Transform Now Plowshares, did after their time in the military: visceral disgust at the realities of war. When asked about this question, Plowshares activist John Schuchardt explains it in the context of resigning his commission at Marine Corps Base Quantico in 1965. He cited "the indiscriminate bombing of the defenseless people of North and South Vietnam, Cambodia, and Laos, meeting the legal definition of genocide." He earlier wrote that, "I did believe in self-defense . . . [but] clearly the US was the perpetrator as defined by all legal principles."[17]

The families of soldiers don't have the luxury of simply watching battles from the distance that TV and news accounts provide. They live in fear during each conflict, and many bury their loved ones. Thus observers may imagine a variety of motivations for Anne Montgomery's actions: legal arguments against certain weapons, her own childhood scars of war, or simply true faith in the God she loved. Nevertheless, the image indelibly remains of her swimming fearlessly in ice-cold harbors to hammer on the nose cones of Trident submarines or Mark II missiles.

Montgomery's persistent, never-extinguished ache for the loss of her beloved brother, who died young in a plane crash during a military training exercise, along with Megan Rice's anguish over the young death of her sister Alessandra, also became part of the two women's shared crucibles of formation. Each of them experienced a sense of the brevity of life, a spirit of "If not now, when?" Rice drove to Washington State to attend Montgomery's trial for the Kitsap-Bangor Plowshares action in part because she sensed, even before they had compared notes on all their life experiences, that there was a deep connection.

Interestingly, a detail from their youths came back to them after many conversations, although both had forgotten it for a time—they met when they were both still teenagers. When Montgomery was a freshman at Manhattanville, the New York City college of the Religious of the Sacred Heart, she visited the Rice family apartment with her close friend Rosemary Sheed, daughter of Frank Sheed and Maisie Ward. Montgomery even attended some of those "heckling" nights for which the Sheed-Wards became so well known. Both women forgot all about these youthful get-togethers until decades later, when Rice visited Montgomery in prison.[18] Rice does not recall any "aha" moment when she knew that she was becoming deeply inspired by Montgomery. They simply fell in together with natural fit, one she considered mysteriously created.

Rice's Society of the Holy Child Jesus and Montgomery's Society of the Sacred Heart are also historically interconnected. Cornelia Connelly, the founder of the Holy Child sisters, was a married music teacher who worked for the Sacred Heart sisters in Grand Coteau, Louisiana, in the 1830s and '40s. After tragic losses of two children, her husband, with personal encouragement from Pope Gregory XVI, asked for an annulment in order to become a priest. She was devastated but agreed. In a complex turn of events that is well worth reading in detail, the pope also requested that Connelly become a Catholic sister. However, instead of following her employers into the Society of the Sacred Heart, she established her own congregation.

The two groups are similar in their commitment to advanced education for sisters, teacher training, and running schools. However, they have distinctions. To name just one example, taking religious names was customary before the Second Vatican Council in the SHCJ and elsewhere, but never in the RSCJ. This difference may sound small, but it says much about other issues and characteristics of the two congregations. After Vatican II, the RSCJ was one of the last groups to put aside their religious habit, whereas the SHCJ embraced the change more readily. Sr. Judith Garson entered the RSCJ in 1958, when they were fully habited and cloistered. Although Garson does not frame the move from habits to street clothes as traumatic the way some others have, she felt it was a defining turn for both groups that affected sisters who had begun their religious lives before the Council, including Rice and Montgomery, in specific ways. News accounts and photos of Plowshares actions may make these sisters seem modern and even radical, but under the surface each remained profoundly shaped by their preconciliar formation in religious life.

The RSCJ and the SHCJ both have historical connections with the Jesuits, as do the Religious of Jesus and Mary (RJM), including common educational foundations in St. Ignatius's *Ratio Studiorum.* This document, which Jesuit historian John O'Malley calls "the Magna Carta of Jesuit education," laid out the teaching program for the congregation's schools.[19] It has not been uncommon since the council years for Jesuits to have RSCJ and SHCJ sisters as spiritual directors and vice versa. The three orders have also often established schools near one another. Both Montgomery and Rice knew Jesuit priest Daniel Berrigan through the Kairos Peace Community that he founded in New York. Judith Garson remembers him as an enthusiastic cook who would invite Rice, Montgomery, herself, and other guests for Mass followed by brunch, creating a New York community that became an integral part of the memories shared at his 2016 funeral.

Neither Rice nor Montgomery ever told their congregations much about their involvement in Plowshares. Both groups knew about it in a general way, but federal laws against conspiracy meant that knowing details and plans would put their superiors or sisters in legal jeopardy. This was a controversial decision, especially when it came to keeping secrets from a provincial, the sister responsible for missioning and granting permission for various activities. Normally a sister would always discuss something as serious as an impending Plowshares action with her provincial, but Rice and Montgomery didn't, thereby protecting their communities.

Garson remembers living with Montgomery in a small community on West 49th Street in New York City in 1980. It was a dilapidated, five-story walk-up tenement, with a bathroom and partitioned showers down the hall from their apartment. The landlord gave the sisters cheap rent in the hope that they would bring a new character and spirit to the place. Montgomery "was wonderful to live with in community. She would do anything at all. She had her priorities very clear, however. The peace work was it, [including] running the risks." One morning in September of 1980, as Montgomery prepared to go out, carrying a small knapsack, she told Garson, "I'm going to be away for a while, and I'm not telling you where. If anybody asks, you can say truthfully that you don't know."[20] Garson had no idea where Montgomery was headed until she read about her arrest in the newspaper a few days later.

Sr. Nancy Kehoe recalls other sisters saying to the provincial, "I hear Anne Montgomery's in jail," and the provincial replying, "Oh, really?" with complete honesty, because Montgomery had not told her superior about her plans.[21]

Clare Pratt, former superior general of the RSCJ, remembers a meeting of the New York and Washington provincial teams in the Greenwich Provincial House when provincial

Ann Conroy received a phone call. When she returned, Conroy said it had been Anne Montgomery notifying her that she was about to participate in an act of nonviolent civil resistance protesting nuclear weapons. Montgomery didn't say what, where, or when the action would take place, in order not to make Conroy complicit.[22]

Later Conroy had a teleconference with the province so that Montgomery could explain why she had done it. This was the first time any of the RSCJ had participated in such a thing, and not everyone agreed with it. Montgomery was grateful for the rest of her life for Conroy's accommodation of Montgomery's call to act on her conscience.

"As much as we could, I think that most of us supported what she was doing," Garson said, although there were individual members who certainly did not approve.[23] The RSCJ held a Mass on March 27, 2011, the night before her sentencing for Disarm Now Plowshares. The Jesuit celebrant asked Sr. Fran Tobin, as a representative of the congregation, to read a "sending" statement co-written by Srs. Kathleen Conan and Paula Toner on behalf of the whole Society.

> Blessing of Anne Montgomery, RSCJ, and the Disarm Now Plowshares advocates being sentenced on March 28th, 2011:
> Peaceful, compassionate God,
>   We come to you in to the midst of a broken world where nations still raise weapons against nations. We ask your abundant blessing on these five courageous disciples who have spared nothing to make the truth, your truth, known far and wide.
>   May their strong voices and willing sacrifice bring us as a people to our senses and give us the courage to insist that our government begin now to dismantle our nuclear arsenals and devote ourselves as a nation to bringing about peace.

> We send you, Anne, on behalf of the Society of the Sacred Heart, to continue your prophetic, educational mission with courage and grace, whether within the walls of prison or without, making known the love of Jesus for our world and all people.[24]

Because of the way she had long structured things—leaving them out of her more minute decision-making processes—they ultimately put up with it. "In general," Garson concluded, "the Society admired Anne to no end. The leadership accepted she would do this because, clearly, it was a call from God in her life. How are you going to say no?" Today an RSCJ intentional community is named in her honor: Anne Montgomery House in Washington, DC. It is a testament to her community's deep respect and love.

Montgomery only received a two-month prison sentence for the 2009 Plowshares action, partly because of her age and health. Over her protest career, she went to prison four times, for a total of three years. Her longest sentence was nearly two years in for Pershing Plowshares (1984) at the Martin Marietta plant in Orlando, Florida.[25] Garson was allowed to visit Montgomery in Alderson prison back in the 1980s and recalls her shock that the environment was always so noisy. "If you wanted to pray, good luck."[26]

Convicted Plowshares activists see the noise of jail and prison as an integral part of the experience of compassion, allowing them to walk with the incarcerated and understand first-hand what they go through. Patrick O'Neill referred to the noise problem years later in his account of his experience at the federal prison in Elkton, Ohio: "As someone with eight kids who also worked in a newsroom on deadline and at many media venues, I am good at blocking out background noise. But in here, the noise of voices bounces off the walls and can be intolerable . . . just another hard part of jail and prison life."[27]

Fr. Louis Vitale wrote from Lompoc Federal Prison, north of Los Angeles, "TVs are loud and almost always on. The noise can be horrific, even through the night."[28] Fr. John Dear wrote from jail in North Carolina, "The past 24 hours have been awful—the noise, the television, the yelling . . . Frankly, the combination of these factors in these close quarters seems to me a modern-day torture. I can no longer think straight. I can't hear myself think. I find it hard to pray. Instead, I lay on my top bunk with the Bible open and read page after page from Isaiah, the Psalms, the Gospel of Mark and Paul's letter to the Romans."[29] Lynn Frederikkson, a fellow activist incarcerated near him, Dear wrote, chose solitary confinement, typically a punitive measure, as a way to escape. "She is at the other end of the building in solitary confinement, so that she can be free of the cigarette smoke and the constant noise."[30]

Literacy advocacy was also an element of activists' jail time. Reading and writing was a consolation for so many Plowshares activists. However, many of their fellow prisoners couldn't read or write. Garson was impressed by observing the way Anne Montgomery taught women she encountered in prison and how after her release she completed further training in adult education in order to serve even more effectively when she was inevitably arrested again.

Montgomery engaged not only with inmates but also their families, some of whom were recent immigrants. In an April 3, 2011, letter to Megan Rice, she described a walking meditation she did in prison that she compared to "another kind of pilgrimage." Walking in a circle, she would spiritually enclose the women and their anxieties within her contemplation.[31] At the end of her two months in prison in 2011, she went by her own request to a halfway house for women in Tacoma, Washington, founded by Bill Bichsel, SJ, and other members of the Tacoma Catholic Worker community. Being there gave even more people from their group a chance to visit. Finally, she was paroled to house arrest in the home of her lawyer Blake Kremer.

Declaration of Conscience
Easter Sunday, 1984

It was the final retreat of the Pershing Plowshares group in Lakeland, Florida. They were planning what participant Patrick O'Neill called a "spectacular" Easter Sunday action on May 22 at the Martin Marietta plant in Orlando. Now known as Lockheed Martin, it built the Pershing II missile, a modern, mobile system that everyone in the nuclear command pipeline knew was designed for a preemptive first strike. This interfaith group was organized by Phil Berrigan and led by Anne Montgomery, who along with O'Neill and Paul Magno, were the Catholics. Jim Perkins was Buddhist, Todd Kaplan Jewish, Tim Lietzke a Quaker minister, and they were joined by two secular peace activists, Christin Schmidt and Per Hengren. They hammered on Pershing II missile parts. Then they formed a prayer circle and sat next to the patrol road for forty-five minutes before being discovered and arrested.[32]

Thirty years later, on Easter Sunday 2014, O'Neill and Magno returned to the scene to plant peace lilies in honor of the two who had since died, Anne Montgomery and Phil Berrigan. O'Neill recalled Montgomery's testimony in federal court. Looking for a place to swing her little hammer, she told the jury how she found a soft spot in the well-constructed weapon, "and I took my hammer, swung it, and saw a dent reflect in the light as I laid my hammer down."[33] O'Neill "was moved that our jury was faced with the task of having to find a small, soft-spoken, humble nun guilty of serious charges for making a single dent in a piece of metal."[34]

The activists prepared a statement together that Anne Montgomery read aloud in court:

> *In a time of the militarization of thought, of oppressive silences and twisted words that call the Pershing—offensive in speed, range, accuracy—a "defensive" weapon, we decry these realities; we express our desire to repent of the deeper violence that "secures" power and property while it bankrupts the spirit of a nation pledged to a welcome for the world's oppressed and to life, liberty and happiness for all. We act as a prayer that our hearing and vision be healed, that those we call "foreigner" and the invisible poor of our world may be seen, recognized and named our sisters and brothers, that we be led out of the darkness of despair and apathy into the light of hope.*
>
> *We act in hope that this Passover may be a new liberation from the consumer lifestyle that enslaves us; from the fear and false securities that paralyze us; in the conviction that, in the midst of multiplied and impotent words, we must risk our bodies to conquer despair. We hope that, in a vulnerability open to the power of God, we can be healed of our violence and, empowered by love, break through the walls that divide "friend" from "enemy."*
>
> *We act in love, in this Easter, this "dawn" of new life: responsible love—recognizing our relationship to these weapons which we must transform, to their creators, all of us in our shared violence and apathy, to their victims who cannot act; communal love—conspiring, breathing together, that we may be one, East and West, North and South in a more human and faithful world; obedient love—enfleshing the prophets' command, "They shall beat their swords into plow-shares and their spears into*

> *pruning hooks; one nation shall not raise the sword against another, nor shall they train for war again."*
>
> *In choosing to disarm our own fear and to say NO to one weapon at its source, we celebrate the renewal of life; we choose the way of love that we and our children may live.*[35]

Both Megan Rice and Anne Montgomery were aware of their abundant privileges, especially being able to visit when Montgomery was in prison. They were conscious of what their ages, educations, and statuses as nonviolent sisters "bought" for them in terms of special treatment when incarcerated. They weren't watched as much. After their sentences ended, because they were retired and had full financial support from their communities, they didn't need to pass criminal background checks for jobs the way younger people who had to support themselves would; they were able to handle the complications of life with an arrest record. White privilege, as we will see soon, also figured in significantly. All of these elements combine to make them ideal for the work of protest, arrest, and mission within prison, and both saw it as their duty to offer this contribution when many others could not. Montgomery's words, written to Blake Kremer, sum it up:

> I have been on a journey, a pilgrimage, since 1980, hoping to follow more faithfully the nonviolent journey of Jesus to Jerusalem. He offered stories and images to his disciples to describe his way of speaking truth to political and religious authorities in solidarity with those who were voiceless and in need of healing from a sense of helplessness and fear. I offer three stories from my own journey.
>
> The first, distant geographically from Bangor, comes from a journey to Basra, Iraq, between the two Gulf wars. In the maternity hospital I stood beside the bed of a woman

who knew she would give birth to a baby without a brain. Helpless to console her, I was then shown a room with its walls plastered with unimaginable photos of deformed infants, never before experienced in Iraq, the result of contamination by the depleted uranium used to harden US tank shells in the southern battles. This is nuclear war, the use of insidious weapons of mass destruction that pollute wherever they penetrate: infants, our own soldiers through contact with destroyed tanks, the water, the earth and its growing things in whatever way they are mined or used in a blasphemous effort to control and dominate creation.

The second image comes from another pilgrimage, this one a five-day walk to Guantanamo in 2005 where we vigiled, fasted, and prayed at the last gate we could reach. At night we could look down on the lights of the prison where human beings were tortured and guards dehumanized. A friend had compared torture and nuclear weapons as two forms of fear-creating dominance and control, the ability to go to a yet higher level of violence in the case of resistance. The nuclear weapons on our undetectable Trident submarines on patrol and stored at Bangor are such a threat, as more devastating conventional weapons are created and used.

The so-called Vision of the Space Command states bluntly that the have-nots of the earth will come to claim a just share of the earth's resources and, therefore that our military might must control space as well as land and sea. The have-nots of the Middle East and our own nation look for a different vision, the one suggested by the prophets: Without a vision the people perish. As we scattered sunflower seeds on our 4-hour walk through the base we hoped to embody the hope that the vision would be realized through the nonviolent resistance and active love of ordinary people.

The final image is of other lights as we entered [the Strategic Weapons Facility Pacific, or SWFPAC]: the blazing

artificial lights over the bunkers, but beyond them, the
gentle, growing, changing colors of dawn offering life and
hope, seemingly fragile, but unconquerable. This vision
echoes the lines from Ezekiel on our statement which challenged us to transform the dead hearts of stone to hearts of
living flesh. This is the journey, first within my often selfish
and fearful heart, and then finding that the change comes
not from me, but from the power of the loving and healing
Spirit of Christ, the beloved community in which we act,
and the larger community of Puget Sound and those worldwide who struggle without such support, those deprived by
our wars and military budget of a human way of life.[36]

Her reference to the "beloved community" is common in
Plowshares circles. It came up during the trial of Rice and
her companions, including in her sentencing statement. Although the term predates him, Martin Luther King Jr., pop-
ularized it in 1956 when celebrating bus desegregation in
Montgomery: "The end is reconciliation; the end is redemption; the end is the creation of the beloved community."[37]

Plowshares' enduring connection with Montgomery was
clearest when Michael Walli and Megan Rice accepted the
Resistance Award from the Nuclear-Free Future Foundation
in 2015, on behalf of all three in Transform Now Plowshares. Lakota activist and actor Milo Yellow Hair, who
presented the award, looked directly at Rice from the po-
dium. With tears in his eyes and his voice breaking with
emotion, he told of visiting Anne Montgomery in prison
when Molly Rush of the original Plowshares Eight took him
to meet her. "It was a little bit like your grandmother being
in jail. Beautiful, kindly. . . . You remind me so very much
of Anne Montgomery."[38]

In 2011, when Montgomery knew her cancer was incur-
able, she moved to California. She wrote to Rice that it "was

another way of making a journey both 'home' and to find new energy to continue in this stage of life."[39]

To honor Montgomery's work in prison, the memorial card for her funeral had a photo from "freedom day," her release from SeaTac prison near Seattle, Washington. Wearing a gray sweatshirt, white prison-issue trousers, and holding her cane, with a simple wooden cross around her neck, she had a beaming, relaxed smile as she received a bouquet of pink rhododendrons. It was May 26, 2011, and she would live only fifteen more months.

Knowing her friend was dying and thus feeling she had to bring it up now or not at all, Rice decided to ask Montgomery how she could do a Plowshares action herself. What would it take to work with a group, pray together, train together, and eventually participate in a full way? How would a person even begin to prepare?

Montgomery's response was typical of her warm but taciturn style. With conviction, she told her friend, "*See Greg.*"

CHAPTER FIVE

Two Veterans Turned Warriors for Peace

"Greg" was Gregory Boertje-Obed, who, along with Michael Walli, would join Megan Rice in the Y-12 action. They became a team that were often good-naturedly referred to by folks in the movement as "MGM" (which we'll use occasionally for shorthand below as well).

The Call of Conscience

He was born Greg Boertje in 1955 in Iowa. He changed his last name in 1993, when, upon getting married, he and his wife Michelle Naar both added Obed, "servant of God" in Hebrew, to their surnames. Boertje-Obed joined the ROTC in order to pay for college at Tulane University, giving him a start in the same US military war machine that had formed others in this book who later became pacifists. As a graduate student at Louisiana State University, he studied psychology. At the same time, reading peace magazines and books about faith made him aware of the social justice issue of nuclear weapons.

Boertje-Obed started active duty in the military in 1981, at age twenty-six. After basic training, he became a medical service officer in the Army, as he said in his trial testimony, "trained to fight and supposedly win a nuclear war."[1]

It didn't take long for Greg to become disillusioned. "The regiment, the hierarchy, the obedience. You just obey, you don't question. In the training course we were taught about nuclear weapons, and we were taught to do this, do that. Ten things to do if a nuclear explosion goes off near you. They did not want people to ask any questions, just accept it. Just be numb. Mindless."[2]

Meanwhile, he was part of a Bible study group near the military base, studying on his own and learning about Dorothy Day. Her peace vision clashed with his war training, and he couldn't reconcile the two. "I read the Bible . . . with a group that said you should take it seriously. When it says, 'Love your enemy,' it's hard to get around that. You don't kill somebody that you're trying to love."

Boertje-Obed reached a turning point during a field exercise involving a nuclear attack simulation. "They said, 'Take this seriously,' and we had to wear these gas masks. We were told that this was a biological nuclear chemical training exercise. We'd have to wear this mask for an hour, then take it off. Two hours, then take it off. Three hours, take it off."

Although he was a lieutenant and therefore could give orders to the medics, he noticed that they refused to do the mask training exercise. Instead of reprimanding them, he thought about it and then tested it. He soon he understood why they disregarded the masks. "I got a severe headache from the mask. If I had to wear this mask in a real situation, I was going to die. I could not just go along with this sham that this mask is protecting me, or us."

By the summer of 1982, he knew this had to end. Boertje-Obed told his superior officer that he could no longer shoot a gun or participate in military activities. The officer helped him apply for conscientious objector status. To his surprise, no one tried to stop him. Now he reasons it was because the nation wasn't at war and there were too many officers anyway. He said there also does seem to be respect from some in the military for people who try to report dutifully, but conclude as a matter of conscience they cannot.

This offers important insight into the work of conscience. If we learn to heed a well-formed conscience (through humble and discerning prayer, study, and engagement with a respected community), we will often discover that those around us try to act in good conscience as well. We should not assume that all others are ignoring their own consciences or uninterested in avoiding evil or doing good. This is why we are called to speak up when it is right to do so. It is healthy to give our companions the opportunity to consult their consciences and respond as their best selves. By heeding the call of our own well-formed consciences faithfully, we can inspire others to do the same.

Boertje-Obed received an honorable discharge in 1982. He traveled to Central America with friends to do human rights work in Costa Rica, Nicaragua, and Honduras. "At the time, our government was demonizing Nicaragua and helping to foster attacks on civilians there."[3] He then came back to the United States for graduate school. At Louisiana State University, he focused on the Bible and peace studies. Eventually he began reading the work of Daniel Berrigan. Berrigan's writing transformed Boertje-Obed, who signed up for summer courses with him at Loyola University New Orleans in 1983 and 1984. While looking back on this time when writing from Leavenworth prison in 2014, Boertje-

Obed recalled what Berrigan taught him in New Orleans: "He said in many ways our lives inside prison are similar to our lives outside prison. We try to study the Bible and pray with others, develop community or fellowship, promote non-violence, and be of service to others."[4] Berrigan's lessons from the early 1980s sustained him in the early 2000s.

During Berrigan's classes, Boertje-Obed also read the work of German Lutheran theologian and pastor Dietrich Bonhoeffer, a World War II martyr whom many Plowshares activists cite as a specific inspiration. Bonhoeffer is best remembered for a theology that urges action instead of "cheap grace," which he describes as "grace without discipleship, grace without the cross, grace without Jesus Christ, living and incarnate."[5] After two summers of Dan Berrigan's classes, Boertje-Obed approached the priest about participating in a Plowshares action.

As Steve Kelly, SJ, and others have always made clear, you can't simply go looking for a Plowshares circle and join it. If you live your life a certain way, you and the people of Plowshares (remembering that there is no formal organization per se) will find each other. Plowshares activists keep an eye on newcomers connected to the Catholic Worker, *The Nuclear Resister*, the Nevada Desert Experience, SOA Watch, and other like-minded groups. When it seems appropriate, they may invite these newer ones to venture deeper after a thoughtful process of growth and discernment. So Boertje-Obed signaled he was willing, but Berrigan also had to agree he was ready. By this time, they considered each other friends. They spoke together often after class, and Berrigan sometimes came to Boertje-Obed's Baton Rouge group house for meals.

Boertje-Obed was open to going anywhere, so they agreed Jonah House in Baltimore was the best choice. After he arrived, Boertje-Obed fit in immediately. He learned to paint houses, as all Jonah House members of that era did. The work was plentiful in Baltimore and flexible enough to let them work part of the week and still be available for rallies and demonstrations.

Boertje-Obed said the planning of their first action together was more of a spiritual than a logistical process. First, they chose the target, a submarine production facility owned by a company called Electric Boat at the naval base in Quonset Point, Rhode Island. Then they performed a close examination of why they were doing what they intended to do. He says now that while some members of the group did fear going to jail, his only fear was that the plan wouldn't work.

After a false start, the group carried out the action, named Trident II Pruning Hooks, on April 18, 1985. They carried hammers, spray paint, and blood. They also brought along the document "A Call to Conscience," an indictment of Electric Boat. They spray-painted "Dachau" on missile launch tubes. Everyone in the group was arrested and convicted on charges of breaking and entering and malicious destruction of property. Boertje-Obed served time in jail but was released during the summer.

Boertje-Obed's next Plowshares action came in January 1987, at the Willow Grove Naval Air Station, north of Philadelphia. Dubbed Epiphany Plowshares, the group of four also included Lin Romano, and two priests, Dexter Lanctot and Thomas McGann. Under banners reading "Seek the Disarmed Christ" and "Swords into Plowshares," the group left an indictment of first-strike policies and did some damage with ball-peen hammers. The Navy valued the property damage at a million dollars, which Boertje-Obed says was impossible with such small tools. Naval investigators even placed Plowshares on a list of international terrorist organizations—one that included Greenpeace as well.

Epiphany Plowshares was notable for requiring four trials; the first two ended in hung juries, and the third resulted in a mistrial. According to Plowshares chronicler Michael Gallagher, the priests accepted a deal from the government after the second mistrial. At the fourth trial in September, 1987, Boertje-Obed was convicted of conspiracy, trespass, and destruction of property. He issued a statement instead of showing up to his sentencing and then went underground. He explained his disappearance in a letter to the court: "Although resistance can continue in prison, going underground is a direct way to say no to the criminal courts which safeguard the bloody crimes of our government. In a short while, I hope to witness by non-violent direct action and will wait to be arrested."[6]

True to his word, he resurfaced on Easter Sunday 1988, when he, Phil Berrigan, and two others hammered and poured blood on the USS *Iowa* in an action known as the Nuclear Navy Plowshares. Boertje-Obed was convicted of trespassing and served twenty-seven months in prison. He received many letters of support, one of them from Michael Walli.

"True to Himself"

Michael Walli was seven years older than Greg Boertje-Obed. He had grown up in a large farm family in Michigan and gone off to war at nineteen. Walli served two tours in Vietnam, earning five medals, including the Bronze Star. Still, much like Louis Vitale, Anne Montgomery, and Phil Berrigan, his personal experience of war caused him to dedicate himself to peace.

Walli has many dear friends and a strong community in Catholic Worker circles, but he also lives with the scars of Vietnam and has transformed tragedy into something meaningful. When asked to describe him, Rice said, "He's true to himself." She noted his deep and consistent integrity.[7] Another admirer noted that on the stand in court he referred to himself as a Christian mystic, and several friends agreed that it seemed accurate. When asked to clarify the mystic part, Walli replied that he has a consistent vision of earth and of heaven.

> I have all sorts of revelations, that sort of thing, sure. Our action that we did, we did communally. We didn't think of ourselves as dreaming up an agenda that originated with any one of the three of us. We all believe that communally we were in alignment with the will of God and human affairs.
>
> Jesus and Mary don't have any nuclear warheads in heaven. They don't permit any torture up there. Everybody's needs, such as they are in heaven, everybody's needs are perfectly satisfied. There's no war. No violence, no threats, no vulgarities, no armaments industry, no abortion industry, no pornography industry, no brawling politicians, no threats, alienation, they let not the sun go down on their wrath, no hostility year in and year out.
>
> Did that answer your question?[8]

Walli believes in the rule of law, a principle he laments that our leaders flagrantly trample. He believes nuclear weapons are illegal because they target civilians. In Vietnam he similarly saw the US military disregarding the rule of law by targeting civilians. Then he came home to observe this failure to protect civilians in the intrinsic workings of the nuclear-industrial complex.

When Walli introduces himself, including on the witness stand during the trial, he'll frequently say that one of his first jobs was to be a terrorist for the US government. He recalls as a young man of eighteen, with the Vietnam War raging, that he faced a choice.

If they draft you . . . they'll put you right in infantry training, they'll ship you right off, and you're statistically more
likely to come back home dead in a body bag. And they'll
bury you in the township cemetery and every Memorial
Day the high school marching band will go out to the
cemetery and play patriotic music at your gravesite. And
the Veterans of Foreign War and the American Legion will
put an American flag right beside the government-supplied
grave marker. On the other hand, if you enlist for three
years, you have the option of asking for noncombatant
training, that way you'll be more statistically likely to survive this Vietnam War.

So he joined the Army and asked for a non-combat position.
　Walli qualified as a sharpshooter on two guns and was
sent to Vietnam in early 1968, where his first job was at the
Army Support Command in Da Nang. Because of his non-
combat request, his tasks included burning classified documents. In the Office of the Provost Marshal, he handled
what he called in court "a lot of matters concerning death,
like a suicide of this one captain from Georgia."[9] He said
he overheard discussions of the B-52 carpet bombings in
the Phước Long Province. The situation crackled with all
the craziness everyone had warned him about, half atrocities
and half banalities. To decompress, he spent a lot of down
time at the beach. Always strategic, he became a good typ-
ist so he could see more of the inside of an office and less
combat during his two tours.
　In November 1969, Walli was on his second tour of duty
in Vietnam. He was at a base near the Cambodian border
when it was attacked from all sides by Viet Cong troops.
When it was over, his jobs included sorting through human
remains and then typing up the body counts. The scene was
similar to the stacked bodies Phil Berrigan had witnessed in

Germany. Walli tried to do his work with emotional distance, but simply couldn't handle it.

He tried to reconcile the happy USO performances the soldiers sat through, featuring Bob Hope full of reassurances that Nixon had an exit strategy, or Neil Armstrong talking about how beautiful Earth looks from space, with US bombings he witnessed with his own eyes. In his courtroom testimony, he said this about his conversion to peace:

> [In April 1968] I was listening in to an Armed Forces Radio broadcast from Monkey Mountain at Da Nang where I was then stationed. And the news came that this US southern agitator from Atlanta, Georgia, Dr. Martin Luther King, had been slain in—right here in Tennessee, in Memphis. So I had kind of misgivings about what I was about. Because in the aftermath of his martyrdom, they're talking about some of his values of nonviolence, condemning the atrocities and the killing of the—he condemned the Vietnam War. He said that the United States was ruled by misguided men with guided missiles. He had all sorts of—he condemned nuclear weapons. It was incremental. I was, like I say, not a scholarly person. But bit by bit, you know, misgivings came into my mind.[10]

Walli was discharged in 1970, but he improbably reenlisted in 1971, perhaps because it was all he knew and there was no home to return to. Without explanation, he then almost immediately went AWOL, following a pattern of heavy drinking and resisting orders, quite possibly all symptoms of what we now call post-traumatic stress disorder. Perhaps because he earned five medals and because he had voluntarily reenlisted before walking away, nobody had the will to prosecute him. The Army discharged him honorably.

For the next seven years, Walli experienced strong symptoms of PTSD. He was emotionally and physically absent from his family and began some personal travels. He held several jobs—shipping company duties in Chicago, sea merchant work in Alaska. Periodically he checked into Veterans Administration hospitals, where he received various combinations of therapy and drugs.

His life only began to make sense again when he began studying the Bible on his own in the late 1970s. After reading the Gospel of Matthew, he felt a miraculous change. In some testimonies, including during his Knoxville trial, he has said he was born again.[11] He moved to Chicago and became a dedicated social justice volunteer, working in homeless shelters and food banks. He also joined anti-war protests that aligned his pain with his growing and sharpening conscience. He has occasionally been portrayed as a drifter by some journalists, but this wasn't accurate. It is more precise to say that his wanderings were similar to the journeys of the early saints. In court for Transform Now Plowshares, he said, "We're citizens of heaven. Our loyalties are to the one to whom the word of God tells us, all authority in heaven and on earth belong Jesus Christ. I am a citizen of heaven. I travel here and there. I told the journalist that I am a missionary, but he insisted on calling me a drifter."[12]

In 1987, Walli went to Washington, DC, to protest the CIA's funding of the war in Nicaragua. He wanted to visit the Vietnam War Memorial, a long, dark wound in the earth covered with names of the dead. It won many awards for its designer, Maya Lin, who was still a student at Yale when she created it. Many soldiers say it speaks to them in a way that the standard "guys with guns" monuments do not, although one of those was erected nearby to appease a small group of traditionalists. Walli volunteered at the Center for Peace Studies at Georgetown University, where he met the anti-war activist Richard McSorley, SJ. With a famously spiky personality, McSorley was best known for protesting the presence of ROTC on Georgetown University's campus, and as we saw earlier, he was invited to join the Catonsville Nine, but declined. He would often stand on the steps of Healy Hall—an iconic Gothic revival building on Georgetown's campus—wearing a large sandwich sign asking, "Should We Teach Life and Love, or Death and Hate?" McSorley introduced Walli to the Dorothy Day Catholic Worker house that he had helped establish and got him writing letters to prisoners of conscience. One of them was Boertje-Obed.

If you read enough of the Plowshares literature, sooner or later you'll find stories about clown suits that involve both Michael Walli and Greg Boertje-Obed. On June 20, 2006, the two men, along with Fr. Carl Kabat, all donned such circus attire and entered the intercontinental nuclear missile Minuteman III launching facility, Echo 9, at Minot Air Force Base about one hundred miles northwest of Bismarck, North Dakota. They hammered on the lid, hung a banner reading "Weapons of Mass Destruction Here," the name of their action, on the front gate. On the silo lid they painted the words "Disarm Now" and "Nuclear Weapons Are a Sin," a paraphrase of McSorley's well-known "It's a sin to build a nuclear weapon," an oft-repeated line he even used as the title of a book.[13] After about forty-five minutes, they were arrested by about twenty armed guards. As they were handcuffed face down, they sang "Peace is Flowing Like a River."

They named their action Weapons of Mass Destruction Here Plowshares, echoing a persistent point made by activists that the United States is the biggest global offender in hiding WMDs. A khaki green t-shirt that Rice often wears and is popular in Plowshares circles has the "Weapons of Mass Destruction US Tour" on the back, with a list of thirty military bases, depots, and test sites housing the weapons.

A United States map on the front has blood-red markers on almost every state: "We Found Them! They're closer to home than you think."

Kabat told lawyer Bill Quigley that the three of them were "fools for Christ." He said, "Court jesters were often the only ones who could tell the truth to the king and not be killed for it! To [people who don't care about nuclear weapons] we are nutballs, but we are doing the best we can to stand up against these evils. My feeling is do what you can do about injustice, then sing and dance!"[14] After they were found guilty, a federal judge in Bismarck sentenced Kabat to federal prison in Greenville, Illinois, for fifteen months. Walli received an eight-month sentence and went to federal prison in Duluth, Minnesota. Boertje-Obed received a sentence of a year and a day, initially went to federal prison in Duluth, and then was transferred to federal prison in Sandstone, Minnesota.

"A 7.5 Billion Dollar Death Factory"

Walli and Rice first met at the Resistance for a Nuclear-Free Future gathering, held over the weekend of July 3–5, 2010, at Maryville College, about forty minutes by car from the Y-12 National Security Complex. It was the thirtieth anniversary of three entities: the Plowshares Eight, *The Nuclear Resister*, and a Wisconsin-based environmental and peace action group, Nukewatch. There was a trespass action at Y-12 during this gathering, and John Schuchardt and Michael Walli were among those arrested. Groups at Maryville College had supported the Plowshares movement going back thirty years, and MGM would meet there together with faculty and students in February 2013 while awaiting trial for their July 2012 action. After the 2010 Y-12 event, Walli would sometimes travel on the Washington, DC, Metro (subway) with Rice, who also lived there, educating riders about nuclear weapons.

In late 2011 and early 2012, Plowshares activists embarked on a series of discrete discernment meetings as they considered an action at the Y-12 facility in Oak Ridge, Tennessee. Steve Kelly, SJ, noted that they had to be careful who was invited, because even people sympathetic to the mission might be pricked by conscience to notify authorities. They couldn't just come out and say, "Hey, do you want to go to a meeting and help plan a Plowshares action?"[15] Some meetings opened with words such as, "Are you planning to act?"[16] This could be followed by study discussions, for example of the International Court's opinion on the illegality of nuclear weapons, or books such as Daniel Berrigan's *The Dark Night of Resistance*. Meetings could also include life sharing, understanding where activists saw themselves in terms of prayer, discernment, and action.

Some were involved who later dropped out, an understandable and natural part of the process. Finally, Rice, Boertje-Obed, and Walli—MGM—remained. They discussed the passage from Psalm 118:22-23, "The stone the builders rejected has become the cornerstone. By the Lord has this been done; it is wonderful in our eyes." After meditating on the Psalm, they found it applicable to government plans to build a uranium processing facility for "modernized" nuclear weapons. Modernization may sound like a good thing, but it can make nuclear weapons smaller, lighter, and easier for terrorists to purchase and deploy. In a talk for the Resistance for a Nuclear-Free Conference at Maryville College in Tennessee, Ralph Hutchison said, "We don't say 'bomb plant'; we say 'uranium processing facility.' But it's a bomb plant."[17] Writing from jail in September of 2012, two months after their Y-12 action, Boertje-Obed explained that they considered Y-12 a "7.5-billion-dollar death factory." Meditating on how Jesus himself was the cornerstone, he wrote:

> A thought that came to us was that the builders of nuclear weapons have rejected the teachings and example of Jesus. Our leading was to seek to act in the tradition of Plowshares actions, to bring hammers and blood, and to attempt to hammer on a cornerstone of a building used for making nuclear horror weapons. We knew that a recent structure was built that was intended to be a counterpart to the proposed [Uranium Processing Facility].
>
> Our intention was to reject nuclear weapons as a cornerstone of our national policy by symbolically and actually hammering on a cornerstone of the new building. We also intended to explain that our action was a rejection of the US role in the world. We knew that our nation functions as an empire that viciously oppresses weaker peoples around the world. Nuclear disarmament and rejection of imperial oppression are both necessary for justice and life.[18]

He concluded, "We give thanks for the miraculous leading of the Spirit, which is how we understand the action occurred. If God can raise people from the dead, then God can lead people past forces of death to continue the process of transforming structures of death to become structures for life-enhancing purposes."

Ellen Barfield is an Army veteran like Walli and Boertje-Obed, and her time in the Army, including duty in both West (at that time) Germany and South Korea, showed her the excesses of US militarism with its hundreds of bases worldwide. Beginning in 1985, post-college, she became an anti-nuclear weapons activist, first challenging the Pantex nuclear weapons assembly plant outside Amarillo, Texas. She and

Megan Rice, who had met earlier, both developed their activist experiences separately at SOA Watch in Georgia. Barfield, who had left the Army sixteen years earlier, represented Veterans For Peace and sometimes served on the SOA Watch board. She recalled how, before 9/11, hundreds of SOA Watch protesters would march onto the base, which was open to the public as most military bases were before the attacks in New York, Pennsylvania, and Washington, DC. There are photos of long lines of people walking the two-lane road inside Fort Benning through the secondary gate that was the route closest to the actual school.

To remove protesters efficiently before they could get to the school, guards put them on buses and transported them across town for temporary detention. There the protesters received "Ban and Bar" letters, which military base commanders anywhere can issue at will to keep the recipients off the base for a specified period or indefinitely. Still, some protesters simply turned around and went right back in.

After 9/11, though, city authorities in Columbus, where Fort Benning is located, contacted SOA Watch before a planned November 2001 action and asked them to refrain because of 9/11. The protesters claimed a right to continue, especially with their long history of nonviolence. SOA Watch took it to court, and a local administrative judge agreed with the protesters' claim of peacefulness, concluding that they had a right to be there. However, once it became impossible to walk onto the base without going under or over a fence, this was considered trespassing, a more serious charge. Although Barfield continued to protest at the base, she never breached the fence after 9/11.

Rice did cross the fence, however, with a group of others. She ended up in front of Judge J. Robert Elliott, known among protesters as "Maximum Bob." He was a criminal judge, not the friendly administrative type that SOA Watch usually encountered, and he had no time for humanitarian activists or any other left-wing shenanigans. Elliott had gained notoriety in the 1960s for forbidding Martin Luther King Jr., and his peaceful protesters to march in Albany, Georgia. But his most astonishing gesture from the bench, one that led most of his obituaries when he passed away in 2006, was overturning the conviction of Lieutenant William Calley for the one of the greatest atrocities of the Vietnam era, the 1968 My Lai massacre, where a company of US soldiers shot up a Vietnamese village, slaughtering more than five hundred civilians, including children. Elliott's decision was overturned on appeal.[19]

Barfield and Rice first met over the phone back when Rice had lived at Jonah House. Someone mentioned Dr. Larry Egbert, and Rice remembered knowing him when they were children. When she picked up the phone to call Egbert to say that his name came up, it was his wife, Ellen Barfield, who answered the phone. A new friendship developed, and Barfield soon joined many of the planning meetings for Transform Now Plowshares. As a member of the support, she prayed with them. In fact, it was her hand-baked loaf of bread with a cross marked into the dough before baking that Rice, Walli, and Boertje-Obed carried with them into Y-12 and eventually offered to share with the guard who found them.

Whole wheat.

CHAPTER SIX

Into the HEUMF

MGM—Megan Gillespie Rice, Gregory Irwin Boertje-Obed, and Michael Robin Walli—approached the Y-12 National Security Complex, in Oak Ridge, Tennessee, at about 2:30 a.m. on Saturday, July 28, 2012.[1] Walli points out that in Catholic devotional practice, July is the month of the Precious Blood.[2] Their action was timed to protest plans for a new 7.5-billion-dollar bomb manufacturing plant to be known as the Uranium Processing Facility. They targeted the current structure, the similarly named Highly Enriched Uranium Materials Facility (HEUMF). Frida Berrigan, author and a daughter of Liz McAlister and Phil Berrigan, wrote that HEUMF "sounds like a noise Winnie the Pooh would make falling out of a honey tree."[3]

The government claimed in 2010 promotional literature that Y-12 existed only "for the safe, secure, and efficient storage of highly enriched uranium and special nuclear materials."[4] It is not a nuclear reactor, but it houses all of the highly enriched uranium our nation needs to manufacture nuclear warheads. Its fifty-year design, touted it its virtual tour, may not sound impressive, until you realize that Y-12

96

itself states that most previous facilities were built with only a ten-year lifespan in mind, perhaps leading the curious to wonder, "And *then* what is supposed to happen?"[5] Also, its promotional literature claims that the facility is built to withstand natural disasters such as earthquakes, which sounds fine until you realize that Japan's Fukushima Daiichi Nuclear Power Plant was also built that way, and it obviously didn't make it. This seemingly planned obsolescence, with a need for continual renewal built into the plan, thus justifying a contracting industry with costs that have spun out of control. "Our 'crime,'" the three wrote from jail in 2014, in an open letter to *The Nuclear Resister*, "was to draw attention to the . . . unconscionable fact that the United States spends more on nuclear weapons than on education, health, transportation, and disaster relief combined."[6] Yet despite these expenditures, alarming video evidence exists of deterioration and neglect, including broken infrastructure, water damage, mold, and lighting issues.[7]

Crossing the Blue Line

Someone—no one in Plowshares will name the person, to protect her or him from prosecution—drove them in Rice's old Subaru wagon to the parking lot of the Oak Valley Baptist Church, a historically black congregation next to a subdivision that abuts the patrol road surrounding Y-12, at about 2:30 a.m. In backpacks, they carried twine, matches, candles, a small sledgehammer, a regular carpenter's hammer, red bolt cutters, spray paint, a black flashlight with a beam partially obscured with duct tape, pre-printed banners, a paper hand-fan that said NO DRONES! NO NUKES!, photocopies of the "Statement for the Y-12 Facility" that opened this book, Ellen Barfield's loaf of bread, cucumber and sunflower seeds, six baby bottles filled with blood, Greg Boertje-Obed's Veterans For Peace ID, three small Gideon New Testaments (two with Psalms and Proverbs), and one copy of the Holy Bible, New Revised Standard Version. Of special note was the blood. The artist and activist Tom Lewis asked that his blood be drawn after his death, to be used at a future Plowshares action, and when he died in his sleep in 2008, someone complied.[8] He had been a part of the Baltimore Four and the Catonsville Nine, among many other actions, and the idea of throwing his blood posthumously was just the kind of poetic thing an artist of his stature would do. Philip Berrigan wrote in his memoir that it was a lawyer, Philip Hirschkopf, who first suggested convinced him that blood should be part of these actions.

The night sky was clear with a 75 percent waxing moon that would be full three nights later. It had been so hot during the day, up to ninety degrees, that even at that wee hour it was tiringly warm at seventy-five degrees. The three very slowly covered a distance of about a half-mile from the parking lot through a small subdivision and then across some fields leading to woods forming a ridge next to the facility. As they approached the first fence at the edge of the property in the darkness, Boertje-Obed made an opening with the bolt cutters. Rice stepped through, officially trespassing on government land, and the other two followed.

This breach moment of civil resistance is a central part of any action. As Assistant US Attorney Melissa Kirby, one of MGM's prosecutors, put it during a court case related to a different protest action, "The government has no issue with demonstrations. The issue is crossing over that blue line."[9] Although it might seem logical to assume that the three activists were nervous or fully afraid, participant after participant in Plowshares actions reports feeling calm, assured, deliberate, and sometimes even stronger in the conviction that this is a right and proper choice. John Dear, who is still a Catholic priest, but at the time of his action was a Jesuit, opened his memoir *Peace Behind Bars* with a meditation about this moment: "Once I step across the line, my life will be changed forever. There is no going back. I start walking. There. I've done it. I am now officially, illegally, on government property. . . . I am breaking the law. I have just walked across a downed fence onto a military base. I keep on walking."[10] Activist Bill Frankel-Streit commented, "There's a certain surrender into it, like jumping off a cliff. After that, it just flows and you're along for the ride in a very real way."[11]

Boertje-Obed slowly led the way up the ridge, going first and flanking with Rice in the middle so they could keep an eye on her and make sure she didn't tire due to a very mild heart condition she'd had most her life. They spread out to avoid detection and angled to the right to soften the incline, but there was still a risk that she would become overtired without someone to occasionally lean on. However, Boertje-Obed had asked her to practice for some weeks before this, and she had done so diligently. Now the three hiked steadily, arriving at the top of the ridge an hour later at 3:30 a.m., their destination in view. Rice was a bit winded but gratified; the rest of the journey that Boertje-Obed now led was downhill. As they continued, they saw vehicles below, and they heard a guard dog bark, but not in alarm. They expected this. Rice had already decided that if she were attacked by the guard dogs, she would not resist. As a biologist and lifelong lover of animals, she had no will to ever hurt a dog, and she could accept being maimed if it came to that. When pressed on this point, she almost seemed to welcome it, but it's also possible to believe a dog might sense that and not try to harm her. Walli has said in many contexts that he would happily have died for Rice that night, and he considered himself her protector. She has said on more than one occasion that he was her guardian angel.

They reached the next fence, this one fortified with barbed wire and festooned with a sign proclaiming "Danger: Halt! Deadly force is authorized beyond this point."[12] As if in response, they took their time at this point, and carefully spray-painted words at the base in all caps: "DISARM. TRANSFORM. PEACE NOT WAR." Then they splashed blood over the words. They hung a banner on the fence, "SWORDS INTO PLOWSHARES SPEARS INTO PRUNING HOOKS." Again, Boertje-Obed cut through the fence and, with Rice slowly leading, they passed through. Before moving on, they hung a banner on the other side reading "Never again," featuring a painting of the Fat Man bomb dropped on Nagasaki.

The next fence had some non-functioning motion sensors, and they reached it at 4:15 a.m. They reached and cut through the final fence at 4:29 a.m. In red spray paint Boertje-Obed wrote, "WOE TO AN EMPIRE OF BLOOD." Walli sprayed in black, "THE FRUIT OF JUSTICE IS PEACE." Both had the characteristic paint dribbles that are now a feature of their iconic witness, often reproduced as a t-shirt popular among peace activists. Rice wrote, "DANGER: NUCLEAR CRIME ZONE." They splashed more blood over their words, hurling it high on the walls so that it dripped down in thin rivulets, a framing cascade. Although MGM could not have known this, seven of thirty-eight cameras were not working that night, including some where they stepped through, and many of the motion sensors had been inoperable for months.[13] Whether you call it contractor ineptitude, the Holy Spirit, or pure luck, they remarkably walked through areas where no one should have been able to even enter. As Rice explained it, showing incrementally with her hands at each step, "We were able to get this far, this far, this far, this far, and [then] do in probably 15 or 20 minutes what we thought we ought to do, quickly," expressing her surprise at how it all unfolded so straightforwardly.[14]

In that short time, they each used one of the hammers to chip at the base of a guard tower that looked like a bland and awkwardly designed castle turret. Boertje-Obed later wrote, "After a few blows, the wall began to crumble. After a few more strikes, the hole widened. A short while later, Rice came with her tiny hammer and swung a few times. The wall continued to crumble."[15] By "wall," he means a corner of the concrete, not the entire structure. The entire damage was only about a foot high and half as wide. Recalling Psalm 118:22, about the stone the builders rejected becoming the cornerstone, they chose a stone in the corner of the building to heighten the symbolism and increase the witness of their action.

At this point they were tripping alarms inside the guard station, but operators initially dismissed them as false. Dan Zak explains that Y-12 had over two thousand false alarms every twenty-four hours, mostly from animals and weather.[16] None of the cameras that covered their zone were working. Zak writes that they even heard the banging and hammering, but dismissed it as construction. Y-12 was spending $150 million a year on security, yet not picking this up. The activists also happened to have started their hammering during a shift change in security personnel.[17] By now they heard a vehicle approaching but continued. They could hear a man's voice, but it was indistinct. Walli spray painted "PLOW-SHARES, PLEASE, ISAIA," but was not able to finish the H before officer Kirk Garland stepped out of his Chevy Tahoe.

Garland wasn't even supposed to be there, but he was covering for another guard during the last two hours of his shift. He confronted the three trespassers without pointing a weapon, recognizing them immediately as peace protesters, based on his twenty-one years at the now-closed Rocky Flats nuclear weapons parts plant near Denver, where such activists, including prayerful Catholic sisters, had been common intruders.[18] Rice folded her hands together at her chest and bowed to him. This is a typical greeting she uses in many situations as a global sign of peace. Then she asked him to please listen to their message. Following Rice's example, Walli and Boertje-Obed bowed to him as well. Walli handed Boertje-Obed a candle, held one himself, and lit both. Rice broke off some of the bread and offered it to Garland. Walli offered him a white rose. Garland calmly refused both.

Garland followed protocol at this point. He told them to keep their hands where he could see them and to make no movement. "How did you get in here?" he asked them.[19]

"God led us here," said Boertje-Obed. Then Walli handed Garland the "Statement for the Y-12 Facility" that opens this book, as Boertje-Obed read it aloud.

Some details of what followed are unclear. Garland is adamant in interviews that he did exactly what he was trained to do. *Don't be a hero. Wait for backup.* Garland did exactly that, and called for backup, as he said in his court testimony. Officer Chad Riggs arrived in another SUV five minutes later, although the response, according to Garland, could and should have been quicker.[20] In contrast to Garland's calm, Riggs asked Garland to cover him with his weapon so that he could put on body armor, and then after he did so, he told Garland to suit up as well, and Riggs covered him.[21] He drew his gun and called for more agents. Two officers arrived and placed the group in plastic handcuffs and leg restraints.

After viewing security video later, everyone from superiors to lawmakers praised Garland for responding so calmly to the situation. It was obvious to him that they were peace protesters, and it was clear that at least Rice, a slight woman in her early eighties, was not a physical threat. He responded well, according to both his training and observations.

However, Officer Riggs later testified in court that—according to his years of training and instincts as an officer—Walli *did* seem like a threat. He separated Walli from the other two and put him in more secure plastic cuffs. The story changed as it was retold, and some began to suggest that Garland had not taken the danger of the situation seriously enough.

That night, more officials and vehicles arrived as the entire nuclear facility was locked down. The three passed the time by singing "This Little Light of Mine," "Down by the Riverside," and "Peace is Flowing like a River." Later the plastic handcuffs were exchanged for metal ones, and the group was taken to the county jail for booking.

"They've Got Us. We Did It!"

The next morning, Rice made her one phone call to Ellen Barfield, who was at Erik Johnson's house. Barfield remembers her saying with great joy, "They've got us. We did it! We did everything we wanted to do." Barfield later recalled, "When I took Megan's first call from jail and heard her elation that they had gotten to exactly where they wanted and done all they had planned, it was clear the blessings of God or the universe had again supported the work of disarmament, as so often has happened with Plowshares actions."[22]

The news filtered through Plowshares circles all the way out to California, where Anne Montgomery lay dying at the RSCJ's Oakwood Retirement Center. Friends told her that the action succeeded. Although it is not clear who did so, it might have been Ann Conroy, RSCJ, the then-provincial whom Anne Montgomery called before she entered the GE plant in King of Prussia back in 1980. Montgomery had a sign on her door at Oakwood that said, "No visitors, please" (because, as she told Clare Pratt, RSCJ, "I need to prepare for death"), but she made only one exception, and that was for Conroy. Whoever told her the news, Montgomery was deeply consoled that Transform Now Plowshares had carried on such a major piece of her life's work.

PLOWSHARES SACRAMENTS: BOOKS, CRIME TAPE, AND OTHER OBJECTS

Plowshares activists commonly bring Bibles to actions, sometimes to read the relevant passages from Isaiah and Micah and other times simply to show in an easily recognizable visual cue that they come in peace. In some cases, they also bring other books to the site in order to be able to use them in court. For example, during the Transform Now Plowshares trial, Greg Boertje-Obed brought Christian Idolatry/ Christian Revival *by Kurt Greenhalgh, who is a member of the Loaves & Fishes Catholic Worker in Duluth. "I chose to hold up that book," Boertje-Obed stated, "because the writer is a friend who lives in Duluth and the book describes how nuclear weapons are a modern-day idol. The Bible includes passages that speak of the need to break idols, such as when Moses broke apart the golden calf [the Israelites had constructed] when he was away on a mountain."*[23] *Although the court tried to prevent it from being admitted into evidence in an effort to limit anti-nuclear conversation and focus on trespass and sabotage, its very existence allowed lawyer Bill Quigley to ask him about it, and allowed him to answer.*

In the Sacred Earth and Space Plowshares II action in 2002, Dominican sisters Ardeth Platte and Carol Gilbert brought Francis Boyle's book The Criminality of Nuclear Deterrence *and left it on the site so that it would be entered legally as evidence. The prosecution's objection to it in Platte's court statement was sustained the first time, but it was eventually admitted. The Kings Bay Plowshares 7 left Daniel Ellsberg's* The Doomsday Machine: Confessions of a Nuclear War Planner *at their site.*[24]

The Transform Now Plowshares group strung red crime scene tape at their scene that said "DANGER, CRIME." At other actions, the tape has been the more familiar yellow, and it usually says "CRIME SCENE, DO NOT CROSS." At the Naval Submarine Base in King's Bay, Georgia, Clare Grady stood behind this type of tape holding a poster: "The Ultimate Logic of Trident is OMNICIDE." Below her feet she had spray-painted the words, "Love One Another," over a heart. The crime scene tape was strung across a vehicle loading area, an indictment of the entire facility as being an illegal, immoral producer of weapons of mass destruction. They also strung it on model missiles.

Other objects that activists sometimes bring are rosaries and photographs. At Weapons of Mass Destruction Here Plowshares, Greg Boertje-Obed placed a framed photo of his young daughter atop a missile silo, along with a copy of the Declaration of Independence, the Constitution, and international condemnations of nuclear weapons. Bill Frankel-Streit remembers an unusual and sacred object from the ANZUS Plowshares action on New Year's Eve 1991 at Griffiss Air Force Base that he performed with his wife Sue: "At that point [in the liturgical year] we were coming out of all the Christmas readings, and it was New Year's morning. There was all this stuff about angels, and so we had gotten this little metal angel blowing a trumpet. We hung it on the fence after we cut it and then went in."[25]

The fences for ANZUS Plowshares were supposed to have been electrified, and they worked both before and after their action, but they mysteriously didn't work right then. "When you go forward in faith," said Frankel-Streit, "the waters part."[26]

CHAPTER SEVEN

Before the Trial

Defendants at trial are often people who have committed a crime but want to avoid punishment. Plowshares upends that dynamic, presenting judges and juries with people who sing, pray, hold hands, and then ask judges to either acquit on the merits—which they believe is appropriate—or convict and punish them. Courtroom dynamics, normally charged with power in favor of the judge as defendants beg for mercy through their lawyers, change. Things shift, both spiritually and emotionally. Judges may not agree with the defendants, but they are frequently impressed. Jurors—often not allowed to see all the evidence when they vote to convict—are sometimes so moved emotionally when they learn who they sent to prison that they have even sought out Plowshares activists and asked forgiveness.[1]

MGM never denied the charges, insisting their actions were just. Instead, their goal was to shift the power and put nuclear weapons on trial, as all Plowshares groups try to do. As Anne Montgomery explained in an interview, "The main issue of this trial is—from our point of view—the criminality of nuclear weapons. . . . You know, the judge wants to stick to the facts . . . such and such laws have been broken . . . period. So that's been very difficult."[2]

To get their ideas in edgewise, MGM wove the legality of nuclear weapons into their answers. For example, on Monday, July 30, 2012, federal magistrate Bruce Guyton initially charged them with criminal trespass. Heavier charges would come later. When Judge Guyton asked if there were questions, Walli said, "I note the charge listed relates only to what I have done and does not include the illegal nuclear weapons production taking place at Y-12." When the magistrate asked Rice, she said, "It is incomprehensible that our charge against the activities at Y-12 is not part of this conversation."[3]

Walli summed it up later for the *Knoxville News Sentinel*: "Nuclear warheads are alien to Jesus' teachings and values. He came that all might have life and have it more abundantly. People should work for life not for death, for peace and not for war, with truth and transparency and not with secrecy and lies. You cannot serve both God and money."[4]

> *What it boils down to, nuclear weapons are designed to do mass destruction. They are going to kill civilians. The intent of killing civilians is a war crime. . . . Just by building [nuclear weapons], you are preparing for the war that will kill civilians.*
>
> —Greg Boertje-Obed[5]

MGM received lawyers on July 30. Bill Quigley, a constitutional and civil rights lawyer from New Orleans and a veteran of Plowshares court cases, was already on their team. As director of the Law Clinic and the Gillis Long Poverty Law Center at Loyola University, he had been honored for his work, including being named the Pope Paul VI National Teacher of Peace by Pax Christi USA in 2003.

Quigley worked *pro bono* because, in his words to the jury, "I'm here as a volunteer . . . because I respect what they're trying to do, and I also respect the constitution."[6]

The magistrate assigned local Knoxville lawyer Chris Irwin, who had represented Walli in his previous Y-12 case. Francis Lloyd, also a Plowshares veteran, represented Rice. In 2010 he represented Jean Gump for entering Y-12 in protest of Trident submarine nuclear warheads. Gump was a laywoman who had previously served a four-year sentence for Silo Plowshares in 1986, including sixty-three days in solitary, for entering Missouri's Whiteman Air Force Base.

Although Boertje-Obed represented himself, technically known as *pro se*, he also had a public defender standing by. Some Plowshares activists choose *pro se* to get more of the argument against nuclear weapons into the official record. They can say things that might get a lawyer professionally reprimanded. Lynne Greenwald of the 2009 Disarm Now Plowshares action on Puget Sound in Washington State explained, "I think by being *pro se*, by speaking for ourselves, we were able to go above the government's desire to have this a case about trespassing, cutting a fence. . . . And with all the restrictions on us for speaking the truth, we were still able to eke out a lot of information about why we were at Bangor and that they are nuclear weapons and that they are a crime against humanity."[7] In that same interview, Susan Crane also explained how *pro se* mediates the difference between the judge's agenda and that of the activists. "We were able to speak what was in our hearts and say things that the lawyers wouldn't be able to say. The lawyers would follow the . . . rulings that the judge had made. . . . I was not particularly interested in following these rules. So I wanted to talk about humanitarian law whenever I could and talk about the necessity defense and get in as much as I could."[8]

However, *pro se* is a privilege of the court, and the judge can also assign stand-by counsel. This happened in the case of Lin Romano and Epiphany Plowshares at Willow Grove Naval Air Station in 1987, an action that also involved Boertje-Obed. The activists considered the judge forcing counsel on them to be a violation of their *pro se* status. They appealed and won. Ralph Hutchison, who chronicled this trial for OREPA and whose words inform so much of this chapter, called Boertje-Obed's public defender "elbow counsel," a common informal legal term.[9]

Boertje-Obed explained why it was unacceptable in the first set of trials to have public defenders represent them and why he accepted it this time:

> In the Epiphany Plowshares trial, we had two hung juries, in which Lin and I were *pro se*, with attorney advisers who could not speak in front of the juries. Our third trial ended in a mistrial also, as the prosecution asked for a mistrial after we spoke out in front of the jury about the strict *motion in limine*.
>
> In our fourth trial, after Lin and I started *pro se*, with attorney advisers, after we spoke out in front of the jury about the strict *motion in limine*, the judge ruled that he was revoking our right to represent ourselves. He appointed lawyers to represent us who were not our attorney advisers. They were working for the judge. We did not cooperate with them.
>
> Lin asked for her attorney advisor to represent her, and the judge said no. Lin appealed our conviction in the fourth trial on the grounds that the judge should have allowed her to choose her attorney. The appeals court agreed, and vacated the conviction.
>
> In the trial that Ralph chronicled, I did represent myself, with an attorney advisor who was a public defender. The public defender worked together with me, and did not

speak before the jury. The judge did not force him to take over my defense, like what happened in the Epiphany Plowshares trial. Thus the situation was much different than the fourth Epiphany Plowshares trial.[10]

Both Rice and Walli pleaded not guilty. Boertje-Obed said, "I plead justified because the building of nuclear weapons is a war crime." When the judge said he had to choose guilty or not guilty, he answered, "I plead for the downtrodden around the world who suffer the consequences of our nuclear weapons." After the judge's third request for a plea, Boertje-Obed said, "I plead for the children who need someone to intervene for them." The judge entered a plea of not guilty.[11]

Although the prosecutor argued they should remain in jail, both Rice and Walli asked for release, with Lloyd adding that Blount County Jail was no place for an eighty-two-year-old. By Friday, August 3, the story had begun to break nationally. It would not become a huge media event until 2015, but it was already receiving more publicity than many Plowshares efforts. Meanwhile, the case to release Rice got stronger. Someone brought her a sweater, a space heater, and a blanket, because she suffered from the cold and was in danger of hypothermia just sitting in the chilly courtroom, let alone jail. She also needed medication that no one provided when she was in jail. This would be just the first of several medical perils she faced, as so many women did in prison.

A number of lay and religious explain their voluntary endurance of these hardships in terms of solidarity with the poor. This identification with the voiceless also became a key talking point in Rice's later advocacy for women of color trapped in the legal system. A few days later she would fall forward and break both wrists. She came to court with her wrists in casts and asked to relocate to Holy Child Center residence in Rosemont, Pennsylvania, for rehabilitation.

Given her previous struggles with the cold and with lack of needed medication, this made sense, but the judge denied it.

The government upped its charge from a misdemeanor to a felony, claiming that the three "did willfully and maliciously destroy or injure or attempt to destroy or injure a structure, conveyance, personal or real property." All three asked for a preliminary hearing, which was set for August 9.

Lawyers for Walli and Rice asked for a detention hearing. Boertje-Obed said he would not accept release even if the judge offered it, because it would require an admission of guilt. Prosecutor Melissa Kirby tried to claim they were a risk to the community, since she didn't get very far with her earlier argument that they were flight risks, but the judge didn't accept this. Kirby reemphasized the risk to their own lives in the kill zone as evidence they were dangerous, calling them "a catalyst for violence. . . . Some other copycat will be shot because of what they did. . . . These people are celebrated by their colleagues—this is a badge of honor. They will do it again. It is escalating. I absolutely believe they are a danger to the community." [12]

Ultimately Kirby contended that their willingness to die for their beliefs itself is violence, but Lloyd countered that the law only considers willingness to subject someone else to harm as a violent act. He said, "Any argument that says any person, simply by exposing him or herself to a risk of danger, makes it an act of violence—makes any protester anywhere surrounded by hostile forces a violent person. It just is not so." [13]

Even though the judge did not accept Kirby's arguments that MGM were violent flight risks, he did wonder aloud why Walli and Boertje-Obed had a history of entering nuclear facilities, even when repeatedly warned not to. He seemed torn, commending both sides for their arguments in a way that made him sound, as Ralph Hutchison noted, much Tevye in *Fiddler on the Roof*.—"On the one hand . . . but on the other hand . . . and on the other hand. . . ." Walli and Rice promised to comply with conditions of the court before their trial. They were released to the Riverside Nonviolent Community House, but Boertje-Obed went back to jail because he would only accept release if the judge would admit that the existence of nuclear weapons constituted a war crime. In the interim, a grand jury convened.

For the hearing on August 9, dozens of supporters crowded in, and some of them reminded the court that it was the sixty-seventh anniversary of the atomic bombing of Nagasaki. The judge said the grand jury had indicted the group on three charges: depredation of federal property, damage or injury to property, and trespass. None of this was a huge surprise. As before, Walli and Rice each pled "not guilty" through their lawyers, and Boertje-Obed offered "a plea for the disarming of all weapons and hearts." The judge asked him again to plead guilty, not guilty, or no contest. Boertje-Obed pleaded "for the transforming of our nation and the world." The judge then threatened to revoke his self-representation unless he "conducted himself properly." Boertje-Obed asked to enter "a creative plea," but he finally pleaded "not guilty." Walli and Rice were freed from the halfway house, and Boertje-Obed again went back to jail.[14]

Bicoastal Solidarity

Meanwhile, in California, supporters held the four-day "Lockheed to Lockup: A Walk for Nuclear Disarmament." They were technically walking with Susan Crane, who had been serving time for her last Plowshares action, back to prison in Dublin, California. But they also supported MGM and Transform Now Plowshares from afar. MGM sent Crane a note of solidarity from Knoxville: "Know that we walk with you, Susan, each day as you carry the Light of Hope, Love, Faith, and Compassion, which is hourly bringing transformation of minds and hearts, beginning with each one of us, of course."[15]

In California, Anne Montgomery grew weaker each day. It cheered her immeasurably to be told that her protégée Megan Rice had made it into Y-12 along with two men she knew so well and trusted so much.

On September 7 supporters visited with Boertje-Obed, who Hutchison noted arrived from the Blount County Detention Center wearing standard prisoner garb and constrained by handcuffs, even though he had never shown the slightest predilection to violence. Although trial was originally scheduled for October 9, the judge continued (delayed) the case until early 2013.

MGM's lawyers tried to have the case recategorized as "complex," because the goal as always was to put nuclear weapons on trial. The judge resisted this but did not yet refuse it. Defense also tried to use the procedure of discovery—one side requesting documents that the other side must produce—to force hearings or even future litigation about the overall legality of nuclear weapons. It would be an uphill and ultimately fruitless battle, however, because Judge Shirley tried, as all judges do, to limit the case to the absolute bare facts: did they enter or didn't they, was it prohibited, and how much damage did they do?

It is a judicial parameter fight that goes back to the early roots of the nation itself. In his introduction to the book *Hammer of Justice: Molly Rush and the Plowshares Eight*, former US Attorney General Ramsey Clark compares the case to that of William Penn arguing for religious liberty in the late 1600s.

We can hear Judge Samuel Salus of Pennsylvania in 1981 echoing Judge Samuel Starling of England in 1670 muttering that the accused is a person of 'cursed principles.' Just as [Richard Browne] told Penn 'You are not here for worshipping God, but for breaking the law,' Judge Salus told Rush, 'You are not on trial for [conscience arising from religious tradition, reading the Gospels, Hiroshima, Nuremberg], you are on trial for the violation of the Criminal Code of Pennsylvania.'

Just as Penn, a lawyer, said, 'The question is not whether I am guilty of this indictment, but whether this indictment be legal,' Molly, a mother, said, 'We're trying to defend life on this planet. . . . We a talking about the morality of nuclear weapons . . . [that is] the heart and soul of our defense. If that is irrelevant, then this court is irrelevant.'[16]

There is also a many-orders-of-magnitude difference between a simple trespassing or even a breaking-and-entering case and the larger goal of MGM convincing the court and jury that they were stopping a war crime, so this legal back-and-forth had serious consequences.

At the detention hearing on September 11, Prosecutor Kirby pushed for Boertje-Obed to return to prison, stating he might not show up for court. She even tried to put words in his mouth about threatening not to show, but the judge stopped her, noting that Boertje-Obed had an unbroken record of appearing in court for all of his dates.

When the judge expressed concern about where Boertje-Obed would stay if he were released, Erik Johnson of OREPA and his wife offered hospitality. The judge, noting that protesters actually *want* to attend trial, then released him with full confidence that he would return. He even added, albeit in loose wording, the larger point that courts tried to wrest from the protesters, "Part of the express purpose of their action is to publicize the production of nuclear weapons."[17]

Boertje-Obed had been in jail all this time, so long that Dan Zak noted some inmates nicknamed him "Y-12." Now, however, he was finally released.

On November 2 they returned to court, and the prosecution entered a motion *in limine*, setting limits for the proceedings. Motions *in limine* were historically problematic for Plowshares, because they prevented defendants from putting the illegality of nuclear weapons on trial. *In limine* prevents defendants from introducing evidence that could lead to a successful justification defense. If granted, the motion would forbid all evidence, even expert testimony, containing any of the activists' most sacred arguments. This would mean they could not include the Nuremberg principles, international law, the necessity defense, the immorality of nuclear weapons, or any conscience arguments, under the overall decision that these things are "not relevant" and that the case is only about trespass and depredation of property or harming the nation's ability to defend itself.

The government dropped the trespass charge in November. However, a grand jury convened in December, adding charges, so two now remained: damage to federal property in excess of $1,000, with its maximum ten-year sentence, and one count of intent to injure the national defense of the United States. This was a stunning change. No one seriously thought the three were in danger of hard time with the earlier trespassing allegation. This new, second charge of sabotage warranted up to twenty-five years.

Some say the threat to charge them with sabotage was an attempt to force a guilty plea, but of course it didn't work. Francis Lloyd tried to have the sabotage charge dismissed because Y-12 is not a national defense facility, meaning that the trio could not have harmed the national defense at that particular location even if they wanted to. That didn't work, either. They were facing charges that could incarcerate them for the rest of their lives.

From the Plowshares Eight to the Present

Ramsey Clark hoped to testify on behalf of Transform Now Plowshares. As Attorney General under Lyndon Johnson, from 1967 to 1969, Clark was instrumental in both the Civil Rights Act and the Voting Rights Act, and he also negotiated the first federal government payments for Indian lands in over fifty years. Clark had been opposed to war ever since he left the Marine Corps in 1946, and he defined his career by a special concern for civilian casualties.

Clark's support of Plowshares went all the way back to the first action, when he testified at the trial of the original Plowshares Eight in February 1981. He based his support in part on his certainty that the United States would use a nuclear weapon again. At Dan Berrigan's celebrity-studded eighty-fifth birthday celebration, Clark had called for a 50 percent reduction in the US military budget, saying, "You can't spend all that money on arms and not use 'em. We ought to save all that money for poor people, everywhere, for food, to help the helpless. . . . It's better to make friends than enemies, but that's totally foreign to our foreign policy. . . . We have to remove a government that permits these high crimes and misdemeanors."[18]

Clark testified for MGM at a pre-trial hearing in US District Court on Tuesday, April 23, 2013. Saying that Y-12's production of nuclear weapons violates the 1968 Nuclear Non-Proliferation Treaty, *which he actually signed on behalf of the United States*, he concluded, "The conduct of the government in this nuclear weapons program is a violation of important treaties that we initiated and signed." He said he believed Y-12's work was at the very least unlawful and perhaps outright illegal, with the former meaning the law doesn't specifically allow it, and the latter meaning the law expressly forbids it. He also agreed with MGM's justification defense, saying their action at Y-12 "was justified and intended to preserve society from destruction by nuclear weapons." He voiced his support for the three, adding, "I agree absolutely with their purpose, which is to eliminate nuclear weapons."[19]

Judge Thapar did seem to wrestle with the difference between a moral and a legal right, asking Clark in different ways whether unsanctioned civil resistance could truly lead to important change. On April 30, 2013, however, he accepted the motion *in limine*, writing, "The Defendants may not present a defense of necessity or justification . . . evidence that the operations at Y-12 violated international or domestic law, evidence that their actions were compelled by the Nuremberg Principles or evidence of their motives."

When the judge accepted the logic of the motion *in limine*, it affected more than just Plowshares' ability to defend itself. It also had a significant impact on what expert testimony jurors would hear. The biggest casualty of the case was the testimony of Ramsey Clark; the judge refused to allow him to testify.

> *"Let's stop pouring our billions into false, impossible security."*
> *Sr. Megan Rice*[20]

CHAPTER EIGHT

"Following Orders" Is No Excuse

On Monday, May 6, 2013, a crowd of supporters in Knoxville, Tennessee surged down South Gay Street from Market Square toward the Howard H. Baker, Jr. Courthouse. They chanted "Transform Now" while drummers kept beat, and actors in papier-mâché big-head puppets marched. Megan Rice said MGM had been "led by a holy, guiding force, and now the spirit of love and hope seemed to be permeating the group."[1]

"The Fire of a Prophet"

The supporters arrived at the courthouse grounds and tried to continue inside the building, drums, posters, and all, but the local police blocked their way. No big-headed puppets allowed! During all this excited, joyful commotion, a city bus went by covered with a full-side advertisement for a local radio station featuring Rush Limbaugh's conservative talk show. It included in huge letters the word "TRANSFORM!," leading Amidon to wonder, "Was this divine intervention? Or did Rush Limbaugh send a bus in support of [nuclear abolition]?" Of course, Limbaugh did no such thing, but it was a light moment in the midst of a parade and demonstration on a very serious subject.[2] Outside the courthouse, MGM supporters held up posters including the image of a whale to represent Jonah House, large cardboard hammers painted with the word "TRANSFORM," and rainbow flags. An acid-green sign said "SWORDS INTO PLOWSHARES" and a yellow one "NUCLEAR BOMBS ILLEGAL." People also carried paper hand-fans that said "NO DRONES! NO NUKES!," identical to the one MGM took into Y-12.

The big-head costumes had been part of an environmental play by OREPA the previous April, about Icarus and the folly of nuclear weapons. Back then they performed the play just outside of Y-12, and now they recreated some of it for the crowd, along with the story of blind people and the elephant. Lissa McLeod said the purpose of using theater in this way is to "move the experience out of the head and into the heart and body. We have done this around issues like nuclear weapons production, the movement for Palestinian sovereignty, ending funding for the School of the Americas, racism and incarceration, and sexualized violence."[3]

Michael Walli addressed the crowd with what an observer called "the fire of a prophet," calling out for US leaders to "send these nuclear weapons back to hell where they came from!" Members of the Nipponzan-Myōhōji-Daisanga, a Buddhist Japanese religious movement, including Sr. Denise Laffan, played prayer drums and chanted their peaceful mantra.

Once the group was admitted to the courthouse grounds, a reporter for the *Knoxville News-Sentinel* interviewed Walli, who said, "This court disrespects the rule of law. It has no respect for the US Constitution. It is about state terrorists' death-dealing activities. The assassination campaigns. The illegal weapons. This false religion of worshiping the bomb." When the reporter asked if he was worried at all about the cynics, presumably those who might convict him, he replied, "It's in God's hands. God's purposes will be served."[4]

Ellen Barfield, who had by now become a spokesperson, expressed concern that the court planned to screen seventy jurors in just one day, working in apparent haste to get the trial over with quickly. A small crowd held hands as Art Laffin led them in singing the names of each of the activists, followed by, "We seek your liberty. We will stand with you until we all are free!"[5]

The city police set up metal detectors to screen the supporters, and sometimes there were long lines to get in. The courtroom galleries were packed. The large number of news media outlets present was so unusual that the judge had to request that seats be saved for them. There was such a crowd that many sat in overflow accommodations in a second courtroom with only a closed-circuit TV to watch the proceedings.

Preparations before Jury Selection

Judge Amul Thapar was on loan to Knoxville for this trial from the Eastern District. A Roman Catholic convert, five years later he would be on the shortlist for the Supreme Court seats that went to Neil Gorsuch and Amy Coney Barrett. Some viewed him as hard-right rather than center-right, but he was also not akin to "Maximum Bob" Elliott, the judge Megan Rice encountered at the School of the Americas protests. For example, that same year as MGM's Y-12 action, 2012, Judge Thapar sided with plaintiffs against police overreach when the federal Drug Enforcement Administration put a GPS on a car without a warrant. It didn't make him liberal, since the case was quite clear, but it may have given some MGM supporters some reason for hope.

Judge Thapar announced his basketball fandom for the Kentucky Wildcats that day, and overall he wrapped up the trial in half the normal time, leaving an impression with many of the journalists and attendees that he was more focused on sports than the case. The prosecution made an early offer before the trial began. If MGM would plead guilty to destruction of government property, they could get out of jail in less than a year. They refused. Although it may sound odd that they opted for a course that would likely result in even more incarceration time, it's typical of how Plowshares people think and work. They are concerned with nuclear weapons abolition first and personal well-being second. After all, MGM had been willing to stand in the free-fire zone of a weapons vault. The spectacle of peaceful protesters serving long terms in prison for denouncing weapons of mass destruction being built with their tax dollars makes a powerful point, one Plowshares people don't feel they can make any other way than by accepting incarceration if the court won't acquit. MGM was committed to putting nuclear weapons on trial and would use the court system as much as they could to accomplish this goal. In fact, they believed it was their legal and moral obligation not to obey or be complicit in criminal wrongdoing by their government.

In his memoir, *Fighting the Lamb's War,* Phil Berrigan wrote, "Jail just makes the most sense to me, and it still does."[6] It tapped into his deeper identity as a former priest, one that many like him who leave the priesthood never lose, "because [jail] is where one identifies with the poor, and where one becomes a spokesperson for their dignity and their rights." Franciscan Jerry Zawada shared similar thinking when he told author Rosalie Riegle in *Crossing the Line,*

"The whole blessed messiness, the blessed chaos . . . I think that's where God is most present. I prefer to stay on the edge of things, to listen to people on the fringes of society. So one of the best places for me to be is in prison."[7]

Plowshares activists often structure their arguments and language on the legal precedent of the post-World War II Nuremberg trials, at which Nazi leaders were convicted of war crimes and crimes against humanity. Nuremberg defendants could not argue that they were just following orders. The Roman Catholic Church has similar teachings. As theologian Drew Christiansen, SJ, has written, "The Second Vatican Council condemned blind obedience to illegal orders as a defense for participation in atrocities, and offered 'supreme commendation' for 'the courage of those who openly and fearlessly resist' such commands. In 2018 two chiefs of the US Strategic Air Command publicly testified that they would have to resist illegal orders and offer alternative courses of action to their civilian superiors."[8]

Post-Nuremberg, knowledge must equal action. On the action of the Transform Now Plowshares, Amidon said,

> All of their efforts were peaceful, legal and necessary attempts to clearly inform the US government of the criminality of nuclear weapons. The trial was also part of this extended action as the court systems were and are equally complicit, and could in fact enforce international law and find that the US government has failed to meet its legal and moral obligations. The spectacle of the government sending nonviolent peaceful protesters to prison for resisting the criminality of weapons of mass destruction made and continues to create a powerful witness and call for transformation. Plowshare activists insist the disarming and decommissioning of all nuclear weapons needs to start immediately. Given our government's unwillingness to comply with the [Treaty on the

Non-Proliferation of Nuclear Weapons], Plowshares people feel their actions are both necessary and legal.[9]

MGM's main defense was a cornerstone of Plowshares thinking: because nuclear weapons unavoidably kill many civilians along with combatants, their creation and use is by definition a war crime. "They take out entire cities," writes Amidon, "target all living things indiscriminately, and poison the land thereafter for many years."[10] It is this reality that prompted Pope Francis to declare about nuclear weapons that "the threat of their use, as well as their very possession, is to be firmly condemned."[11]

Lawyer John Schuchardt, a member of the original Plowshares Eight, developed some of the first Plowshares legal arguments as a public defender in Windham County, Vermont, in the 1970s. When he was in Norristown Prison and Western Penitentiary for his own Plowshares action, he further refined those arguments. During ten years of appeals, they became the legal framework and foundation of subsequent Plowshares trials.

Describing his experience of a previous trial experience for an earlier Plowshares action, Boertje-Obed made reference to the oath one takes before testifying:

> You can't talk about God, you can't talk about the Bible. You can't talk about your religious beliefs, on and on. . . . But the message came to me to turn it on its head when they asked me [to take] the oath in that trial. When you take the stand, you're supposed to affirm or swear to tell the truth, and the whole truth. I had this very clear message that when they asked, I would respond, 'It's hard for me to answer that because this one person here who wants me to take the oath, he wants me to tell the truth and the whole truth. But this other person over here, the judge and the

prosecutor, they don't want me to tell the whole truth. So who am I supposed to listen to?' The judge didn't get real upset. He was just kind of taken aback.[12]

What It Means to Come to Trial in East Tennessee

Jury selection was unusual because Judge Thapar, rather than the defense or the prosecution, asked all the questions. To the deep frustration of the defense, he told the jury that the trial they'd be hearing involved "a notorious case." He never acknowledged, even after one of the defense lawyers brought it up later in a sidebar, just how inappropriate this was.

Six out of seven potential jurors said they had read about the case and thus had quite probably already formed opinions. But it's unlikely that any jury made up of East Tennesseans, who lived in an economy dependent on Oak Ridge, would be inclined to see nuclear weapons as fundamentally illegal.

Of approximately seventy people in the wider jury pool, over half identified as either being veterans themselves or having family in the military. Many had family members or close friends in law enforcement. "Even if we had thrown out all 70 and got 70 more tomorrow," said Ralph Hutchison that evening at a gathering of supporters, "that would still be the pool that we were drawing from. That's what it means to come to trial in East Tennessee." He did think there was a chance that veterans might be open to hearing the ideas the Plowshares defense would rely on, simply because so many knew what their government was capable of. Three of the seventy had engaged in some form of protest, demonstration, or strike in their own lives. It could have been worse; no one in the jury at the trial for Walli's 2010 Y-12 action had any sort of experience of this kind.[13]

CHAPTER NINE

Don't Blame the Thermometer for the Fever

At 8:15 on Tuesday morning, a security guard in front of the courthouse tried to disperse a large, peaceful group of supporters gathered there in a circle. "Y'all have to have a permit," he said, interrupting the reading of Isaiah 2:3-4. One protester answered, in a friendly voice, "The first amendment . . . the US Constitution is our permit, sir." Michael Walli quickly added, cheerfully, "I've got a copy!" The group was allowed to remain.

Judge Thapar was difficult to analyze. On the first trial day, May 7, 2013, he mentioned Martin Luther King and Mahatma Gandhi, professing admiration. "You can't tell me that Martin Luther King or Gandhi didn't disrupt things when they were nonviolent. They're extremely admirable people that did, in my opinion, great things but still disrupted. I mean, that was their goal, right?"[1] Then the next day, May 8, lawyer Chris Irwin told the judge he took the liberty of bringing along a copy of Gandhi's autobiography, hoping to discuss it with him, and Judge Thapar mentioned having some "perspective" on Gandhi through a grandfather and great-grandfather.[2] This may have been an allusion to the fact that his maternal grandfather had campaigned with Gandhi for India's independence.[3]

During sentencing, he also mused aloud on the difference between protesters and terrorists. As Boertje-Obed's wife Michele Naar-Obed said later to a journalist, "The judge was really struggling with the difference between the letter of the law and the spirit of the law."[4] During these on-the-record musings, however, was he sincere? Or was he just trying to *seem* fair? If prior law couldn't give him room to make a distinction between pacifists and terrorists, then why couldn't he do it himself, while keeping the legacy of Gandhi in mind?

Judge Thapar may have felt limited by *stare decisis*, the principle of respecting the precedent of previous judicial rulings. Although it has a broad, apolitical meaning, it can be used to describe a more specific practice of many politically conservative justices. Thapar had been clear in the past of the importance to him of two principles dear to many conservatives: textualism (interpreting the meaning of a law by the ordinary and objective meaning of its text) and originalism (interpreting a law according to the way its original authors intended it). In a 2019 talk at the University of Notre Dame, Thapar said, "[Supreme Court Justice Antonin Scalia] believed that a judge's role was to interpret the law as written. . . . Even when he ruled in a way he did not like, he did so because he believed the judge's role was to interpret the law honestly and perfectly, not as a judge wished the law to be."[5]

Even though the judge warned the defendants not to bring up the illegality of nuclear weapons as a defense, a supporter writing for OREPA noted that the prosecution seemed to do it for them: "[The prosecutor] told the jury the banners read 'Transform Now' and the paint on the wall said 'Transform Disarm.' She [Kirby, one of the two prosecutors] described the banner on the fence, a bomb encircled by fire and the words 'Never Again.' Jurors heard the area was roped off with crime scene tape by the defendants. In the loveliest twist of all, she noted that Megan, Michael and Greg, once they were in custody, proclaimed their anti-nuclear agenda to 'their captive audience,' the security guards who apprehended them."[6]

When lawyer Chris Irwin opened for the defense, he was able to address the same topics because the prosecution had brought them up in their comments about the peace activists. "We've heard the mention of reasonable doubt. It can be as large as an elephant or as small as a mouse. There's no size requirement for reasonable doubt. . . . What you'll find throughout the evidence is they had white roses. They had Bibles. They had banners. They had signs. What they didn't have was grenades. They didn't have machine guns. They didn't have dynamite. They weren't dressed in camouflage."[7]

Was the prosecution actually sloppy in bringing up details that the judge had excluded from the case? Or was it strategic? Courtroom observers that day differ on the interpretation. It might have been carelessness, and it might have helped the defense, but it also might have been confidence that an East Tennessee jury would find peace activists irritating.

When the assistant district attorney asked Steven Erhart, the Y-12 operations manager, "How many times has the United States deployed a nuclear weapon?" the manager asked her whether that was the question she intended to ask, which prompted her clarification, "How many times have they been deployed and activated?"[8] Many MGM supporters noted that this was helpful to the prosecution and therefore highly problematic. The answer to the original question would have been tens of thousands of times, having deployed them all over the world in aircraft, submarines, and silos and detonated them in many tests. But the answer to the rephrased question, as prompted by Erhart, was only two. Erhart's prompt of the attorney for the prosecution offered the strong impression of a witness overstepping his role and a judge allowing it to happen.

Defense lawyer Bill Quigley felt that Ramsey Clark could have contradicted much of this testimony, adding to his frustration that the judge had refused to allow Clark to testify. Quigley said as much during a break. Then Judge Thapar told Quigley that he didn't seem to grasp the issues, leading John LaForge to ask whether the judge was deliberately pretending not to understand.[9]

When Quigley began cross-examination of Erhart, he went right to a problem that some supporters also noticed. The prosecution's case hinged on the supposed security that Y-12 provided the nation and the world. If it was so secure, then Quigley asked why its cameras didn't work for six months. Did Y-12 tolerate a "culture of complacency"? Erhart said he preferred "normalization of the deviation from the optimum. They became too comfortable with things not working than they should have." To many this sounded like Orwellian newspeak, wordsmithing to paper over serious issues. *Washington Post* reporter Dan Zak, who observed the trial, noted that by this time a juror had fallen asleep.

Officer Chad Riggs, the second guard on the scene, also testified. Some MGM supporters felt his testimony hinged on feelings rather than facts, which further complicated things for the jury. For example, Riggs said he put plastic handcuffs and leg restraints on all three activists and made them lie face-down on the ground because he sensed danger.

He said he separated Walli from the others because "through my training and experience as a law enforcement officer, I had a gut feeling he was the most dangerous one." Riggs said he was sure there was "obviously some sort of what appears to be blood, human biological material, all over the place." Riggs insisted that he knew it was blood, even though it was splashed high on the walls and, at 4:30 a.m., it was dark. How did he know it wasn't paint or mud?[10]

To be fair, one could argue that Officer Kirk Garland also worked from feelings rather than facts when he concluded they were peace activists and therefore didn't draw his weapon or handcuff them, but he had more of a historical basis for his belief. He had worked at the Rocky Flats Plant in Denver, Colorado, where scores of protesters, including Rice's friend, the Mennonite pastor Peter Ediger, protested for so many years using many of the same symbols. Officer Garland recognized peace protesters from decades of first-hand experience because of their specific paraphernalia, not just by his mere gut feelings. His experience allowed for a balanced and professional response. Yet his superiors criticized his response and praised his colleague for the cuffs and rougher treatment.

When, during cross-examination, lawyer Chris Irwin asked Officer Riggs to describe the weapons he saw, given that he claimed to feel so much danger, he could not actually say that he saw evidence. Defense lawyers replayed video in the courtroom showing Rice bowing to the officers and Walli lighting his and Boertje-Obed's candles. Irwin asked Riggs to point out holes blasted in the side of the building, which of course were not there.

Plowshares activists strategically bring various items onto an action site so that they can be admitted in court as evidence. Amidon notes,

The deepest hope is these items will help us to understand cognitively, spiritually, symbolically and emotionally the immorality and illegality of nuclear weapons, giving us the opportunity to transform our thinking and allow for nuclear disarmament. MAD (mutually assured destruction) and UD (unacceptable damage) are the two major strategies for the use of and defense against nuclear weapons attacks, illustrating the likely omnicidal outcome of the normalization of nuclear weapons and nuclear war. . . . The court's (judge's) failure to allow and consider the full range of our legal and moral teachings is the "legal" nullification and corruption of law and common sense.[11]

Bringing items to a site makes them part of the evidence that a judge cannot exclude, and thus the strategy can maneuver around most judges' desires to keep religion out of the proceedings. Irwin tried to use this to the defense's benefit. He asked Riggs what was written on the hammer, and he read aloud, "Trust God, not first-strike terror weapons." Some thought this was helpful for the defense, but was it? That remains an open question, for these slogans might annoy or even anger some of the East Tennesseans on the jury whose economy was beholden to the nuclear industry.[12]

A Y-12 manager estimated damage caused by the activists at $8,531.67, including fixing the perimeter fence and patching and repainting, with overtime costs thrown in.[13] Boertje-Obed refuted this, remembering his time painting for Jonah House. He noted it only took one gallon of paint to cover a whole room. It was an effective debunking of an obviously padded bill, but he didn't know that some of the repair was also vastly overstated in another way. Two different Y-12 witnesses testified that the fence had been repaired with plastic zip ties. However, Boertje-Obed told Ralph Hutchison and Erik Johnson during a jail visit that he had seen the photos provided by the government, and they were not of the entry point that MGM had used at all. Based on Boertje-Obed's directions, Hutchison and Johnson found the spot, and it was still unrepaired. They took pictures and delivered them to Frank Munger of the *Knoxville News-Sentinel*, who wrote an article in December, after which Department of Energy finally repaired the true breach, five months late.[14] Yet department officials swore on the stand that someone repaired it the day after the action, at a cost of over five hundred dollars.

The prosecution showed Department of Energy Special Agent Ryan Baker strands of cloth that Walli attached to his hammer and asked him to read them.

Agent: 'The United States is the chief—' I can't read that word.

Prosecutor: Is that 'purveyor'?

Agent: Could very well be, sir. 'Of violence in the world today. Dr. Martin Luther King.' 'Every dollar that is spent on armaments is a theft from the poor. Dwight D. Eisenhower.' 'Oppose the culture of death. Pope John Paul II.' 'All war-making preparations in the Middle East represent a major defeat for international law. Pope John Paul II, January, 1991.' 'Peace is the fruit of justice. The Word of God.' 'I surrender all to you, Lord Jesus.'[15]

The prosecution showed Michael's blue hard hat with "UN" printed on the front and unfurled the big banner in the iconic photo that said "TRANSFORM NOW PLOW-SHARES." The courtroom also listened to recordings of the three taken from their phone calls from jail. Jurors heard

Rice say, "We did it to try and heal it, and begin the work of disarmament."[16]

Megan Rice took the stand. Barbara Bartlett, SHCJ, who lived in community with Rice in Washington, DC, in the years after her release, recalled that when Rice had entered the courtroom, "there was an 'almost smile' on her face, while the expressions on the faces of the other two were grave and serious. It was obvious she felt she was just where she should be."[17] She wore a sweatshirt that said I WISH TO LIVE WITHOUT WAR.

When it was time to be sworn in, she asked if in addition to the oath, she could swear on the Constitution. When asked for her birth year, she said, "I was born in 1930, right in the depths of the Depression."[18] This was strategic, to bring in the poor. She wove concern for social justice into her narrative, whether discussing the nature of her religious congregation, her father's work with poor women as an obstetrician, or her mother's research on the abolition of slavery.

She reflected on Selig Hecht, her suspicions that he might have worked on the Manhattan Project, and on her uncle Walter Hooke at Nagasaki. She especially recounted her time at Boston University, learning to handle radioactive isotopes. She explained her years in Africa and then her return to the United States and work with the Nevada Desert Experience.

After she recounted her entry into Y-12 with Walli and Boertje-Obed, she asked to read the group's "Statement for the Y-12 Facility" that opens this book. To her and the defense's surprise, the prosecution did not object, so she was able to read it in full.[19]

Of the many ways to understand the legal strategies used in a trial like this, including the prosecution's supposed earlier fumbles that may or may not have been mistakes at all, one chilling possibility comes to mind. The prosecution could have been so certain of a conviction that its lawyers were not worried about peace messages being read into the official court transcripts. In fact, it could all have been a strategy—somewhat akin to the more cynical interpretation of the judge's invocation of Gandhi—to merely make them seem even-handed. Even if that's the case, though, Rice's reading surely fulfilled one of the many goals of Plowshares in carrying out these actions: to establish through case after case in court after court a history of resistance, occasional legal precedent, and an indelible official record.

Perhaps pressing her luck, which miraculously held, she then asked to read an indictment of Y-12 for war crimes. Now the prosecution objected, but the judge overruled and let her do it. After reading it, she said she felt led into Y-12 by the Spirit of God. She explained why she bowed to the first guard, saying it came from her interfaith and Buddhist impulses. She called it a "very great consolation" that Kirk Garland recognized them as peace protesters, for "one could sense that he saw the scenario that we had created, the message that we had created, the symbols and the labeling of the building with truth. That was what our intention was, to label the building with truth in a very short time."[20]

She said she had heard Garland say "These are peace protesters" on his radio. And as for that big bill for cleaning up their mess of blood and hammer marks, she thought that if this had happened back in Nigeria, they could have gotten a little whitewash and done the job in an afternoon. She said they used their hammers to perform "an act of reconstruction" on the corner of the nuclear facility, but a small amount of cement—not even worth opening a new bag—could have fixed the few chips they made. When she ended her testimony, she stood. As bailiffs led her away, she bowed to each juror.[21]

After the judge dismissed everyone for the day and counsel conferred, Bill Quigley pointed out that "the government has never proven the link between the disruption and the intent to injure the national defense of the United States." In fact, "the proof is exactly the opposite. . . . The security at Y-12 is actually significantly better today than it was the day they showed up. And as a result, the national security of the United States is better today than it was the day they showed up.[22]

The judge agreed with Quigley that the security improved since the incident. But he insisted that didn't matter if they intended to interfere with national security. "All that matters is their intent. So if they go in intending to steal the nuclear weapon, right, and they get shot before they even get into the PIDAS [Perimeter Intrusion Detection Assessment System], they're still guilty. But if they go in and all they intend to do is sing songs, and they actually disrupt the national defense and the whole country's national defense system gets shut down, they're not guilty as this statute is written."[23]

Quigley agreed with this, and they discussed "foreseeability." If even the experts at Y-12 didn't manage to foresee all the security failures that characterized that night, how could the defendants, who didn't work there and didn't know the facility at all?[24]

Some of the precedent in the conversation came from *US v. Platte*, the government's case against Dominican sisters Ardeth Platte, Jackie Hudson, and Carol Gilbert in 2005, which included this passage: "Certainly, the jury could properly infer that defendants intended a disruption like the one they actually caused at the missile site. At the very least, signs on the fence warning that deadly force was authorized against intruders would have alerted them that their entry would elicit a vigorous response."[25]

This initially looked bad for the Transform Now Plowshares case, and the judge said he planned to reread it. But Quigley pointed out that the cases were different. Platte, Gilbert, and Hudson were standing on top of a missile silo when they were caught. "I think [the government] even flew helicopters in that one," he said. They weren't charged with sabotage, but Walli, Rice, and Boertje-Obed, with a smaller-scale action, were. Author and former *Catholic Worker* editor Jim Forest has noted that the charge of sabotage was a worry from the very first Plowshares action, but it didn't happen.[26] Quigley asserted that the government dropped the trespass charge this time in order to set MGM up for a sabotage charge. "If the Courts are in the position to say that anybody who commits any act who wants to get press about disarmament is therefore interfering with the national security of the United States of America, I think [that is] far, far too broad."[27]

Then the court and lawyers discussed the closing of Y-12 for two weeks after the incident, an event which had surprised MGM and the entire team. Quigley pointed out that it was for retraining due to lax security, not because of anything the three did. The judge seemed interested in this line of reasoning. Quigley also said since they had witnesses claiming MGM harmed the national defense, then he, Quigley, should be able to call witnesses saying the opposite for the defense. They also argued over whether civil resistance is by its very nature nonviolent, citing Martin Luther King and Gandhi.[28]

Francis Lloyd tried to get permission for Rice to "testify concerning her belief that the nuclear weapons do pose a present, imminent and impending threat of death or serious bodily injury," something the judge ruled out when eliminating the necessity defense.[29] The judge claimed the defense waived the right to do that, but they hadn't, so he suggested a proffer, meaning putting up a statement for immediate acceptance or rejection. The prosecution immediately objected. This kind of verbal chess typified the whole trial, as the court and prosecution did whatever they could to box in the defendants and keep them from saying anything meaningful about nuclear weapons. Even when the prosecution inadvertently "helped" the defense, it seemed to do so from a position of confidence that overall it would prevail.

Meanwhile, experts filed declarations in support of MGM. Among them, Nobel Laureate Ira Helfand, MD, copresident of International Physicians for the Prevention of Nuclear War (IPPNW) and cofounder and past president of Physicians for Social Responsibility, IPPNW's US affiliate, offered this statement: "If only 100 Hiroshima-sized bombs were detonated over cities the resulting firestorms would loft enough soot into the upper atmosphere to drop temperatures across the globe an average of 1.3° C. The resultant drop in food production would put more than one billion people at risk of starvation. Each US Trident submarine can carry up to 96 W-76 warheads. That means that each of them can create this Nuclear Famine scenario many times over. The US has 14 of them."[30]

Bishop Thomas Gumbleton, a cofounder of Pax Christi USA and auxiliary bishop of Detroit from 1968 to 2006, wrote:

> In 1963, Pope John XXIII, in his teaching document, *Pacem in terris*, made the statement 'In our atomic era it is irrational any longer to think of war as an apt means to vindicate violated rights.' In my opinion, the Just War theory, used for centuries to justify and bless military and war making, disappeared with that one sentence.
>
> Nuclear weapons have been repeatedly condemned. In 1965, the Second Vatican Council ruled out any use of any

weapon of mass destruction. The use of such weapons is a crime against God and humanity. In 1976, Pope Paul VI recalled the use of nuclear weapons on Hiroshima and Nagasaki and identified the bombings as 'butchery of untold magnitude.'

Nuclear weapons are wrong and evil. Resisting such evil is not simply a matter of being responsible citizens. It is a matter of safeguarding and deepening our spiritual well-being. I am convinced that there comes a certain point when evil public policy that cannot be changed must be resisted. People of faith and people of ethics must resist evil. We cannot remain silent. We must resist and say no in whatever way we can to nuclear war, to the arms race which stockpiles and refurbishes nuclear weapons, to the testing of nuclear weapons, and to any step in the process by which the evil is prepared and continued.

Thus the actions at Y-12 of the three individuals facing charges in this matter are consistent with our faith tradition and are praiseworthy actions to resist the evil of nuclear weapons.[31]

Next to testify was Colonel Ann Wright, retired from the Army after twenty-nine years. She was also a lawyer and a decorated former US diplomat who had served as deputy ambassador at embassies in Afghanistan, Sierra Leone, Micronesia, and Mongolia, and a political or administrative officer in Uzbekistan, Kyrgyzstan, Grenada, and Nicaragua. Wright had received the State Department Award for Heroism for the evacuation of 2,500 people during Sierra Leone's civil war, which was the largest foreign evacuation since Saigon. She later became one of three high-profile diplomats to resign (separately) in opposition to the 2003 US invasion of Iraq. The day before the invasion, March 19, 2003, she took the career risk of sending what is known as a "dissent cable" directly to Secretary of State Colin Powell, stating that without UN Security Council authorization, the United States would be in violation of international law. When that was not heeded, she wrote a letter of resignation. Her work since then has been to make up for having supported the military and the government in the past even when she disagreed and to expose untruths. She is now able to say with a full voice, "Don't believe your government, because they lie all the time. I was part of it and I know they were lying."[32]

Quigley chose Wright because she had been stationed in Central Asia in 1991 and 1992, during the breakup of the former Soviet Union. Kazakhstan was one of two places where Russians tested nuclear weapons, the other being an island in the Arctic Circle. After the breakup of the Soviet Union, the United States maneuvered its highly enriched uranium from that region to Y-12 in East Tennessee, and Wright knew the background first-hand. She opened her testimony by stating the immediate danger in Tennessee, and then took the courtroom into more details about the uranium transfer. "We have bombs that can blow this section of Tennessee off the map and pollute the whole east coast, if not the world . . . this is one of the most dangerous places on earth, right here in Oak Ridge, Tennessee. And the probability that it is targeted or will be targeted is very, very high. . . . [F]or me as a person who's spent a lot of my life both in the military and the State Department protecting US government properties, I am astounded at what was going on here."[33]

Quigley asked her, "Do actions by demonstrators and other people who get on to the property, who commit vandalism . . . harm the national security of the United States?" Wright responded,

> Well, the fact that there may be vandalism or something written on a wall does not harm national security as such.

What it does is highlight the fact that security procedures that were supposed to stop that were not there.

But as far as the words being spray painted on a wall or something like that, that doesn't harm our national security. . . .

In fact, I think what has happened is that we are much more secure now, and the people of Oak Ridge are much more secure now, because the vulnerabilities of the security system that should have been in place were found out.[34]

Prosecutor Kirby tried to quiz Colonel Wright on her knowledge of nuclear facilities generally, to expose gaps in her knowledge and discredit her testimony. However, Kirby rambled so much that the judge asked her to wrap it up. Wright did get to testify about the presence of depleted uranium in Kazakhstan in 1994. "The Kazakhstan government was very uneasy about having all of this enriched uranium there, because they really couldn't protect it. And so the . . . decision of the US government was that we would bring that material, if it was okay with the Kazakhstan government, to Oak Ridge, Tennessee . . . to be protected so that it would not be found, as was noted in the statements of both the Secretary of State at the time and the Secretary of Defense, to protect it from rogue elements of the world."[35]

* * *

Under questioning from his standby counsel Bobby Hutson, Greg Boertje-Obed was able to speak about the book, *Christian Idolatry/Christian Revival,* that he carried onto the site. As we saw earlier, part of the purpose of carrying extra objects to the sites of Plowshares actions is to make them admissible in court. The judge did not allow him to read from the book—written by Kurt Greenhalgh of the

Loaves & Fishes Catholic Worker in Duluth—but Boertje-Obed also brought his Veterans For Peace ID onto the Y-12 site, so he was allowed to read its statement of purpose:

1. To increase public awareness of the causes and costs of war

2. To restrain our governments from intervening, overtly and covertly, in the internal affairs of other nations

3. To end the arms race and to reduce and eventually eliminate nuclear weapons

4. To seek justice for veterans and victims of war

5. To abolish war as an instrument of international policy.[36]

Boertje-Obed noted that he didn't take any weapons that could be used to hurt anyone with him in the Y-12 action and that he and his fellow activists sang songs of peace. He closed by testifying that officer Kirk Garland knew they weren't a threat, and even though he never accepted the candles or the bread, he also kept his weapon holstered and even turned his back on them at one point, knowing for a fact that they were peaceful.

When the prosecution tried to emphasize that Boertje-Obed had previously been convicted of a felony, he repeatedly restated it was for a "peace action."[37] After some back and forth, the judge instructed the jury not to use the felony conviction to decide whether he was guilty now. What the judge said couldn't negate what they'd heard, however, and that was clearly the prosecutor's goal. When the prosecutor tried to get Boertje-Obed to say he wanted to eradicate all nuclear weapons, he said clearly, "I want to follow the treaty we have signed as a nation."[38] This would have been Ramsey

Clark's testimony as well, had he been allowed to give it, since he was actually one of the signatories of the Nuclear Nonproliferation Treaty.

When asked if he believed Y-12 was evil, Boertje-Obed returned to the ideas in Greenhalgh's book: "I have introduced this book, which says I believe it is false worship of a false God."[39] He also said that part of their goal was to protest the Uranium Processing Facility that the Department of Energy planned to build right next to the Highly Enriched Uranium Materials Facility where they entered. No matter how much the prosecution tried to get him to say that his goal was to personally eliminate nuclear weapons, he kept coming back to the non-proliferation treaty and wanting the United States to do what it said it would do.

The prosecutor asked if Boertje-Obed had ever considered protesting the proliferation of nuclear weapons in China or Pakistan or Russia. "No," he said, "because I was born in this country, and I feel a responsibility to this country."[40] He discussed different uses of depleted uranium beyond bomb-making. Again, this is a point Ramsey Clark would have made and that Ann Wright did make. She pointed out that the United States retrieved depleted uranium from Kazakhstan, which couldn't store it safely, and they brought it right there to Oak Ridge and Y-12.[41] Depleted uranium itself can also be used as a weapon or to enhance other weapons. First used during the Gulf wars, military scientists have hailed it as the proverbial "silver bullet," capable of piercing the steel armor that protects tanks. It has another nickname, though: the Agent Orange of the twenty-first century. It penetrates soft tissues, causing leukemia and other cancers and leading to birth defects in soldiers' children.[42]

For closing arguments, the prosecution swept past the allegation of damaging United States property. Their real focus was the major charge, "injury or destruction to national defense premises"—in other words, sabotage. The burden on the prosecution was to prove that MGM had "the intent to injure, interfere with, or obstruct the national defense of the United States."[43] The prosecutor emphasized the term *national defense material*, hoping to convince the jury that MGM had interfered with "arms, armaments, and fuel" by shutting down Y-12 altogether.

The defense would claim they did no such thing and that Y-12 only closed to address its abysmal security. That was an international disgrace having nothing to do with Plowshares, other than that they exposed it.

The prosecution kept coming back to intent, with the word *willfully* being key.[44] MGM didn't have to succeed, they just had to try. By using human blood, the prosecution further claimed they contaminated a nuclear site. The prosecution lasered in on MGM's use of words such as *disarm* and *transform*: "That's what they want. They want disarmament. Ask yourself, does that affect the national defense of the United States, their disarmament? Is that their intent? Again, they don't have to actually cause that. Did they have that intent?"[45]

In essence the prosecution was saying that by wanting these things, by saying "never again," and by writing those words on a wall, they should be guilty of intending to *cause* disarmament or guilty of intending to *cause* some sort of physical, immediate transformation. From a First Amendment perspective, it is alarming, because under this broad interpretation, anyone who writes or displays any public words of protest could be found guilty of actually intending to do what the words say. All protest words would become actionable threats.

After one of the prosecutors admitted that MGM used no weapons and threatened no one, he said, "Even if some of their messages are symbolic, that doesn't mean you're not interfering with what they did, you're not obstructing what Y-12 is doing."[46] Under this standard, even picketing outside a facility would be illegal, and elsewhere in the trial this prosecutor granted as much when he told Boertje-Obed that he should have protested at a building set up for that purpose, several blocks from the facility itself. Now the prosecutor claimed that harming Y-12's international reputation was MGM's fault, although of course its own shoddy security was to blame.

The prosecution team tried to discredit Colonel Wright's testimony, saying you don't excuse what a burglar did because a homeowner had lax security.[47] Later MGM's lawyers countered that this is an inappropriate analogy. Instead, one must consider that the burglar enters a house with an intent to steal and do harm, which they did not, and also that Y-12 was no innocent, sleeping homeowner, but a facility charged with global security that failed at its most basic job. Y-12 had enough nuclear material to destroy the world and wasn't protecting it properly. Prayerful people armed with flowers, candles, Bibles, and a loaf of whole-wheat bread were able to defeat its security by simply walking in.

Just as the prosecutor did, defense lawyer Bill Quigley jumped over the first part quickly, tabling the discussion of whether damage exceeded a thousand dollars. Everyone agreed it didn't truly matter. The big deal was count two, whether MGM actually interfered with or harmed the ability of the nation to defend itself and whether their actions rose to the level of sabotage. This was the key point the judicial panel would revisit two years later on appeal. Quigley emphasized this was not a mere "preponderance of the evidence" kind of case, where there is a close judgment call to make.[48] For MGM to be guilty, they must have acted maliciously "beyond a reasonable doubt." Getting their attention on this distinction would be an uphill battle, he knew, as he addressed this jury composed entirely of East Tennessean white people with deep connections to law enforcement, the military, and Y-12. "Now, these folks may not be the most popular folks in town." That was surely an understatement. He went on,

> Some of you may and some of you may not agree with their positions about nuclear weapons or disarmament. You may think they're spiritual. You may think they're socialist. You may think they're idiots. You may think they're prophets. That's not what it's about at this point. At this point, it is, "Has the government proven every element of the crime beyond a reasonable doubt? . . ."
>
> [Y]ou have to be convinced beyond a reasonable doubt that the defendant was aware of a high probability that his or her actions would create this injury, interfere, or obstruct with the national defense of the United States. Carelessness or negligence or foolishness is not the same as knowledge and it's not enough to convict.
>
> So they had to know going in, right? You heard, this is sadly—we could say a comedy of errors, but the stakes are too high to talk about a comedy of errors. They would have had to know that a camera that would have seen them hadn't been working for six months. They would have had to know that the parts for the fence were back ordered for who knows how long. They had to know that different parts of the management at Y-12 weren't talking to each other.
>
> This was a chain of mistakes that were made at Y-12, and was there a high probability that they knew? Could they have known, to a high probability, that they were going to injure or hurt the national defense of the United States? The people at Y-12, who have been there for 20 years, didn't know that. Nobody foresaw that this kind of thing could happen.[49]

Then, using a much better analogy than the prosecution's weak comparison of a burglar breaking into a house, he said:

> Does a thermometer give you a fever? A thermometer doesn't give you a fever. A thermometer shows that you have a fever. I would say to you that these folks didn't cause the fever. They pointed out that we have a fever, and we have a fever at one of the most dangerous spots in the United States, as we pointed out.
>
> So you promised that you were not going to take away anybody's freedom unless the government proved beyond a reasonable doubt every element, and the element that I ask you to focus on is that element. Did these folks show up with the intent to injure the national defense of the United States? . . .
>
> They are against nuclear weapons. They think we ought to disarm. They think we ought to disarm now. That's part of the banners they held up. They believe that. They can't be punished for their opinion about that. That is not that they intended to injure the national defense of the United States, no matter how unpopular or popular their opinion is.[50]

Quigley was careful to put the blame for the two-week shutdown on Y-12 and its shoddy security rather than on MGM who were able to enter in the wee hours of the morning because its security cameras had not worked properly for months. "These three folks can show up any Wednesday at the Piggly-Wiggly in New Orleans and automatically get the senior discount. They would never be carded, right? So when three senior citizens can, with no weapons other than some bolt cutters, when three senior citizens can walk all the way on to a base, then we know we have a problem."[51]

He also reminded them that the truly wronged party wasn't the leadership of Y-12, but Officer Kirk Garland, who had found the peaceful protesters, recognized them for who they were, and did his job.

> And it is a shame, I think, for our whole process, for all of us that Mr. Garland, out of all this, out of all the people from the top to the bottom, who lost their job as a result of showing the problems at this place? Mr. Garland. Was he the one that hadn't fixed the camera for six months? Was he the one who hadn't back-ordered this stuff? Was he the one sitting up in the tower? Was he the different management groups that weren't talking to each other? No. He was the low guy on the totem pole and he got blamed for it and lost his job. And that's a shame. . . .
> So again, don't blame the thermometer for the fever.[52]

* * *

After a recess, Greg Boertje-Obed made his closing remarks. He compared himself and his two fellow activists to the Good Samaritan, seeing victims of nuclear weapons by the side of the road of the US empire and stopping to help. Calling the United States the "sole remaining superpower," he noted that the nation has bases and drones all over the world. Then citing "The Emperor's New Clothes," he said they hadn't harmed the credibility of the US defense, but rather that the facility had done that itself. They were merely like the little boy who said the emperor is naked. "The emperor does not have effective fences. . . . Nuclear weapons do not provide real security."[53]

Next Francis Lloyd, not just a member of the Knox County Bar but also a neighbor to the jurors, spoke. Representing Megan Rice, he reminded the jury that a sense of humor can be helpful in a tense courtroom. He pointed out the misuse of terms during the prosecution's case, such as *breaking and entering*, which was not one of the charges, and also *trespassing*, which the government had already dropped.

> They get all the way beside the HEUMF. They've not encountered a living soul, armed or unarmed. They've not encountered any sort of weapon or tank. First officer from the pro force drives up, and what are they doing? They're standing there. One's offering him bread, two light candles, and then one reads a statement.
>
> Again, foolish? Maybe. Naive? Probably. But if they were intent on destroying or interfering with or obstructing the national defense of the United States, do you think they'd be standing there with a loaf of bread and two candles in a situation in which they've symbolically taken hammers, tapped on a wall, spray painted slogans from the Bible, put blood on?
>
> They're not running away. They comply with instructions. This doesn't look like the manifestation of an intention to interfere with operations at Oak Ridge any more than I look like somebody qualified to play in the National Basketball Association.[54]

Referencing the many thousands of dollars the Y-12 manager and a general said it cost to repair the damage, he reminded them that Boertje-Obed said it should have taken about one gallon of paint and a day of work, and that Rice said it would not have even required one bag of cement. So where did a bill of over eight thousand dollars come from? For one thing, the no-bid process and the well-fed contractors. He went on to declare the whole trial to be about Y-12 covering up its own well-deserved disgrace.

> The shortcomings in security at one of the most dangerous places on the face of the planet have embarrassed a lot of

people. I would submit to you that because they've embarrassed a lot of people, because contracts have been lost, you're looking at three scapegoats behind me.

There's a great many things that are right about our government, but I'll tell you one thing that's wrong about our government. The man who, based on his own experience, recognized—who recognized peace protesters when he saw them, who dealt with them appropriately, is the individual who doesn't have his job today.

The individual who put these three people whom Professor Quigley described as almost certainly qualifying for senior citizen discounts, the man who put them face down on the ground and handcuffed them with tight plastic cuffs still has his job.

Figuratively speaking, the government is asking you to again put these people face down on the ground and handcuff them. I ask that you resist the call of your government to do that.[55]

For the closing argument, the prosecution made an absurd stretch, comparing MGM's peaceful protest at Y-12 to the atrocities of 9/11. Prosecutors asked the jury if just because security got "better" after 9/11, we should now thank the terrorists. Then one of the prosecutors backtracked and said he wasn't calling them terrorists, but of course it was too late. He had deliberately placed that image in the jurors' imaginations. He assured them repeatedly that they didn't have to worry about punishment in this case, as that would be Judge Thapar's responsibility. All they had to do was agree that MGM intended to disrupt the nation's ability to defend itself.[56]

After the jury went out to deliberate, defense lawyer Lloyd called for dismissal or outright mistrial. "We got through an entire trial without any use of the word terror or terrorism, and then counsel in his concluding argument used 9/11, implying a comparison between these defendants and those."[57] The judge tried to note that Theodore had immediately walked that back, but Lloyd wasn't having this transparent fallacy, saying it was too late by then.

The jury began deliberations at 3:39 p.m., and they reentered the courtroom at 6:01 p.m. Megan Rice, Michael Walli, and Gregory Boertje-Obed were found guilty on all counts. All that remained was the sentencing hearing at 9 a.m. the next day.

CHAPTER TEN

"The Greatest Honor You Could Give to Me"

"Festival of Hope" is the name Plowshares activists have given to gatherings they often hold at some significant juncture in an activist's journey through the legal process, especially at a trial or a sentencing. Paul Magno describes them as an opportunity to celebrate the message of the action anew in word, song, and prayer. Such a festival brings in supporters, family, and notable personalities. When possible, the activists attend, if they are not already incarcerated. A festival is also a reunion and a reinforcement of the meaning of the cause. Magno says it "restates the message of the action, renews its hopeful, truthful core and raises the morale of the extended community invested in the action."[1]

Celebrating Hope

Magno remembers a Festival of Hope in Philadelphia before the 1981 resentencing of the original Plowshares Eight. Pennsylvania courts had upheld the activists' convictions but overruled the long sentences of three to ten years imposed in earlier that year. After a vigil at a nearby General Electric facility, the festival continued with folk music from Pete Seeger, Charlie King, Joyce Katzberg, and Reggie Harris. All eight defendants, who were eventually resentenced essentially to time served, were among the speakers.

During that Festival of Hope, a group gathered on Ash Wednesday, March 4, 1981, to watch Anne Montgomery, John Schuchardt, Elmer Maas, Daniel Berrigan, Carl Kabat, Molly Rush, and Phil Berrigan burn items in a metal container to create ashes. Among many items, they burned "this ridiculous indictment" of the court:

"This is 'criminal trespass,'" Berrigan read from a sheet of paper. "Let us burn it for God's sake."

"Amen," said the group. Then he fed it to the small fire.

"This is repeated hammer blows and 'criminal mischief,'" he read from another page.

"Amen!" said the group.

"Burn it."

"Conspiracy," read Montgomery, offering more sheets, some of which she tore up.

"Amen!" answered the others. "Burn it."[2]

The group then carried the ashes to the courthouse to mark one another's foreheads, after which they invited anyone who wished to receive ashes to join them.

There were several small festivals for Transform Now Plowshares, including the street parade that had accompanied them into the courthouse on the day before the trial. Then, on the evening of the first day of the trial, supporters gathered in a version of the Festival of Hope. They sang the Quaker standard "Simple Gifts," and then heard from various supporters. Rice and Walli, who were not yet incarcerated, attended. Walli wore one of his favorite t-shirts, reading "GROUND THE DRONES." Folk musician Charlie King played guitar and led the group in various songs, including the Tom Paxton favorite based on a passage from the book of Isaiah, "How Beautiful Upon the Mountain," adding some new lyrics:

> Marching to Guantanamo
> Or to the Pentagon
> Witnessing to peace in many lands
> Speaking truth to power
> Singing peace in Babylon
> Beating swords to plowshares in your hands
> God knows the courage you possess
> And Isaiah said it best.[3]

King performed in a rich tradition of folk singers engaging the mission of various Plowshares groups. On the first day of the Disarm Now Plowshares trial in Washington State in 2010, folksinger James Morgan offered his original work, "The Battle of the Disarm Now Plowshares," adapted from an Irish folk song.

> I've been a good citizen for many a year
> While they spend all my taxes on weapons of fear
> And now I'm returning, resolved to do more
> And I never will play the quiet neighbor no more!
> And it's no, nay, never
> No, nay, never no more
> Will we take up these weapons
> No never, no more.[4]

Sentencing

The sentencing hearing for MGM took place over nine months later, on February 18, 2014. All three had spent the intervening time in prison. On the day of sentencing, it is common in Plowshares for a group to gather tightly around the defendants with hands outstretched toward or touching either them or their images, to offer a pre-sentencing blessing. As in the previous events, locals provided potluck suppers in churches, activists lit tiny tea lights on a table to make a display of love and light, and old friends convened, many of whom were veterans of past actions.

Outside of the courtroom, Steve Kelly, SJ, and another Plowshares supporter, Libby Pappalardo, held a SWORDS INTO PLOWSHARES banner. Pappalardo had met Kelly and Rice in September 2010, while participating as one of the "Creech Fourteen" in the first action against drones at Creech Air Force Base. Outside the courtroom Kelly said, "We'd like those who are coming into the court today to know that this is about a conversion. An economic and political conversion of all of our resources to go from warmaking to peacemaking."[5]

In their final statements, Walli continued this conversion image, calling their action "lawful missionary work. . . . I committed no crime. I have no sense of remorse or shame . . . I make no apology. I would do it again."[6] Boertje-Obed offered a copy of Martin Luther King's speech "Beyond Vietnam" to the prosecution and jury, and quoted Daniel Berrigan's poem, "Hymn to the New Humanity":

> Guns believe in guns, guns hope in guns, guns adore guns.
> In the new dispensation, these are honored as theological
> virtues.[7]

In her own statement, Rice again recalled her childhood neighbor Selig Hecht and many workers at nuclear weapons plants who couldn't tell their families what they were doing.

The secrecy, she said, was evidence that their work was evil. She compared the United States to the Third Reich and said to the judge, "We have to speak, and we're happy to die for that. To remain in prison for the rest of my life is the greatest honor that you could give to me. Please don't be lenient with me. It would be an honor for that to happen." Then she asked the judge, "May I end with a song to lighten the moment?" The judge agreed, and the sister turned to the gallery to conduct supporters as they sang along:

> Sacred the land, sacred the water.
> Sacred the sky, holy and true.
> Sacred all life, sacred each other
> All reflect God who is good.[8]

Later she led it again outside with supporters who stood in a circle and sang along with her.

The sentencing took place on the seventy-first anniversary of the arrest of the White Rose, the group of young people and their philosophy professor who protested in Nazi Germany and were executed for their resistance. Before sentencing, Judge Thapar mused rhetorically, "Don't you find it a little troubling that Congress would write a law that wouldn't let me distinguish between peace activists and terrorists?"

Activist Clare Grady pointed out a glaring inconsistency between the originalism and textualism that seemed to animate the Judge's career and what happened in the courtroom:

> So today what we heard was a lengthy, lengthy examination of the law, and yet the supreme laws of our land were left out of the courtroom, left out of this trial. The Constitution, Article Six Section Two: 'All treaties, pacts, and protocols that are signed and ratified become the supreme

law of our land; every judge is to abide by them.' And those laws have evolved over the years to outlaw war of aggression; outlaw weapons of mass destruction; outlaw killing civilians; outlaw occupation; outlaw stealing the earth's resources to build these weapons. We are not upholding those laws.[9]

According to the Constitution of the United States, "All Treaties made, or which shall be made, under the Authority of the United States, shall be the supreme Law of the Land; and the Judges in every State shall be bound thereby, any Thing in the Constitution or Laws of any State to the Contrary notwithstanding."[10] So not only was the testimony of Ramsey Clark, who signed the 1968 Treaty on the Non-Proliferation of Nuclear Weapons on behalf of the United States, excluded, but the Constitutional implications of the existence of the treaty were disregarded.

In passing his sentence, Thapar told Rice, who was by now eighty-four years old, "I have confidence you will be living well past any sentence I give you." Of course, he had no way of knowing if she would survive this or not, and he knew she had medical issues during the trial. Was he concerned she could die in prison? As a Catholic, did he have reservations about convicting a sister? He then sentenced her to thirty-five months, or almost three years. Boertje-Obed and Walli received sixty-two months, or a little over five years each.

> *Nuclear weapons and the Rule of Law cannot coexist. . . .*
>
> *Judge Thapar said at sentencing, he wanted to "deter" other activists but he didn't think they did any real harm at Y-12. The Prosecutor said they destroyed the 'mystique' of the 'Fort Knox of Uranium.'*

> *The mystique they destroyed was that Y-12 and Oak Ridge are part of an infallible scheme to protect the country and its citizens.*
>
> —*Anabel Dwyer*
> *Law professor and member of the board of directors,*
> *Lawyers Committee on Nuclear Policy*[11]

The Closing Door

Rice was supposed to serve her sentence at Danbury Prison in Danbury, Connecticut, the setting of the hit series *Orange Is the New Black*, which had debuted on Netflix less than a year earlier. Rice's Plowshares colleague Ardeth Platte was the real-life Catholic activist on whom the show's character Sr. Ingalls was loosely based. Rice began her sentence there in February 2014, but in the middle of March transferred to the harsher Metropolitan Detention Center in Brooklyn while Danbury closed for renovations. Although the move to Brooklyn was supposed to be temporary, she ultimately remained there for the rest of her sentence.

Boertje-Obed went to Leavenworth prison in Kansas. Walli went to McKean federal prison in Pennsylvania. As many prisoners will tell you, there is nothing quite like the sound of that door closing behind you for good. No matter how accustomed an activist may become to the idea of imprisonment for conscience, the door still closes firmly with a metal clang, followed by the click or a lock or the sliding of a bar. John Amidon remembers it well.

> One of the truly threatening and scarring sounds in life is the first time you hear the slam of your cell door closing behind you. In my minimum-security pod, there were about 12 cells total, six cells on two levels. Beginning at one end

of the tier, when the doors closed there was a rapid succession, automatically controlled . . . loud clangs, a threatening, menacing invisible force, rapidly approaching. My cell door violently slammed shut with a deeply disturbing physical and psychological finality.

A visitor or worker gets to go home at night. I knew I would not.[12]

It is final. It is solemn. It is real.

PLOWSHARES SACRAMENTS: CANDLES

Even a single lamp dispels the deepest darkness.
 Gandhi
  Written on the sweatshirt Greg Boertje-Obed wore
  the first day of the trial

Candles are a way to quietly shine light on nuclear secrets that activists believe should be public knowledge. They symbolically dispel secrets, the kind Megan Rice always lamented. The Transform Now Plowshares activists took special care when lighting their candles. They did so at Y-12 after Kirk Garland showed up to arrest them in the early morning dark. Michael Walli had two candles, so he gave one to Greg Boertje-Obed, and then lit them both. They quietly held them as Rice offered bread to the guard and all three waited to be arrested.

On January 2, 2021, people around the world lit candles at dusk to commemorate the Treaty on the Prohibition of Nuclear Weapons entering into force. In 2020, a group at the Pentagon marking the massacre of the Holy Innocents by King Herod (Matthew 2:16-18) sang and used candles to light their way out: "As the sun began to set, we held candles to symbolize Jesus, the Light, overcoming the darkness! The witness concluded with everyone singing 'This

Little Light of Mine' as the community processed down the escalator and into the Pentagon metro station lobby."[13]

The publication Shut Down Creech *in Nevada reported activists making a "Victims of Terror" altar using candles, flowers, and names and photos of some of the child and adult victims of US drone attacks.*[14]

During Hanukkah 2020, Felice and Jack Cohen-Joppa remembered the plight of a prisoner they supported as they lit their candles. "As we continue to work for a peaceful, just and nuclear-free world, we're often not able to know if our efforts make a difference. But still, together, with hope, faith, determination and love, we forge ahead! Friends, we are glad to be on this journey with you . . . let us all continue to bring light into the darkness."[15]

Activist Rosemary Russell writes,

There is in each of us something that responds to a candle burning, and especially so in the dark of a winter night. Whether we come from a religious tradition or not, the act of lighting a candle somehow gives us pleasure, restores us to ourselves, gives us relief and hope. Where all was dark, now there glows and shimmers a little flame. And that flame becomes a symbol of all we hope for, all we long for with all our hearts—health and joy for those we love, food and shelter for those among us who are without, comfort for those who suffer, justice for the oppressed and the coming of peace in a world laboring with the heaviness of conflict.

As we light our candles together, may each of us be filled with the light they bring, and may we reach out to one another in joyful resolve to live into our hopes each day.[16]

Of course, framing darkness as negative and light as positive is a race-problematic trope. Plowshares activists acknowledge this, and many prefer to use more neutral language. The beauty of candles remains, however, and they have always been an integral part of actions in the Plowshares tradition.

> *Give light and people will find the way*
> *Ella Baker, African-American civil rights activist*

CHAPTER ELEVEN

Doing Time for Peace

The title of this chapter comes from Rosalie Riegle's book *Doing Time for Peace: Resistance, Family, and Community,* to honor her brilliant work as an oral historian of this movement. It also conveys how Plowshares activists think about their sojourns in lockup. When they go to prison, they learn to walk with, minister to, and be ministered to by the world's incarcerated poor.

Of course, there's nothing new about going to prison for a just cause. Rosa Parks, Mahatma Gandhi, Dorothy Day, Nelson Mandela, Martin Luther King Jr., and many others have done it. Activist Tom Lewis explained that members of the media often don't grasp it. "They couldn't understand the idea of a spiritual witness and its continuance in prison. This kind of action doesn't really have a political rationale. It does have a spiritual rationale."[1] Bill Frankel-Streit says, echoing Phil Berrigan's words, "Prison heightens the witness."[2] Berrigan himself told an interviewer before the trial of the original Plowshares Eight in February of 1981,

> Americans need to investigate more deeply, of course, the value of prison witness. One person in prison for conscience

speaks out more emphatically against the crimes of state than ten thousand would from the street who are educating for justice and peace. . . . [I]f the state is going to lock up some of its best citizens, what does that have to say about the state? That's the value of the personal conscience, right from the early Christian times down through Gandhi and especially in this country. The prisoners of conscience of this country are perhaps the most notable in the world, and hopefully they will increase in number.[3]

"Deeply Disrespectful, and Meant to Be"

To understand incarceration from a Plowshares perspective, it helps to remember that imprisoned activists are not alone. Doing time for peace brings out the best of their communities. Supporters, from close friends to complete strangers to celebrities, write letters. Many who are near the jail or prison visit. Helpers on the outside are willing to send any book the prisoner requests and the facility will allow. Greg Boertje-Obed noticed that his prison library at Leavenworth had only one book on Martin Luther King Jr., and it was for very young readers. There was nothing else on peace. He requested titles from supporters, however, and by the time he left, the library had a strong collection.

Supporters write to Plowshares activists in prison; it is considered part of the whole experience of the action. Even just sitting in the DC jail, Ellen Barfield remembers getting ten to twenty cards a day around the winter holidays from supporters. Meanwhile, many other prisoners did not even hear once from their families. Rice saved many cards and letters from her times in prison, and they will become part of her official papers when she is ready to donate them.

Sometimes even the people who are part of the system that sent the activists to prison become supporters. US Army

Major General John LeMoyne wrote to Rice at Danbury: "I admire your sincerity, Sister Rice, and even agree with your ideas. We have just chosen different paths to influence change for the better." He also offered any assistance he could, and he signed it "With respect."

Rice responded to LeMoyne,

> Your note surprised me and my fellow inmates and gave us moments of mirth. They especially could not imagine the person who arrested them writing such a note. So it was bitter-sweet once again for me to be aware of my privileged place among so many long-suffering and anonymous women, unrecognized for their valiant endurance of intense pain of separation and often very unjust sentences. You ask kindly if you can be of assistance in any way. Yes, of course, we are all equally responsible to serve humanity. Please read thoughtfully and with time, the attached points. They succinctly state the root causes of world poverty and global desecration in our times. Also, I was asked in our computer class at Danbury Prison if you have surplus army computers to donate.[4]

So the experience is communal, but that does not make it easy. Many aspects of prisons are designed to break a person down. Rice traveled from one facility to another on a freezing cold plane. Guards denied blankets to the women, who wore only regulation white cotton t-shirts and khaki trousers. When they landed it was thirty degrees outside, but they could not have coats. Rice is of medium height but only weighs about 105 pounds. As previously mentioned, decades in Africa also made her sensitive to the cold, so she suffered. When she lost a cap on a front tooth while in prison, they sent her to a dentist to stabilize it, but that was all; she had to put the cap in a box, live with a broken tooth, and wait until release.

Some facilities refuse to send prisoners' medical records when they are transferred, leading to needless charges as prisoners must replicate expensive diagnoses and prescriptions. In Rice's sentencing statement, she decried this element of the capitalist prison system run by private companies, saying, "Imagine the profit accrued."[5]

Longtime Plowshares activist Susan Crane wrote from the Federal Correctional Institution Dublin (California), of her spirit of solidarity with those who suffered. "I am with the woman with a broken arm and no treatment, one who has an earache month after month or an untreated kidney stone." She recalled Jesus' admonition that helping "the least of these" meant helping Jesus himself (Matthew 25:31-46). In prison she pondered the corporal works of mercy up close and personally: to "give drink to the thirsty, welcome the stranger, clothe the naked, take care of the sick, visit those in prison." She saw women who had very little nevertheless tending to one another's needs. If poor, incarcerated women could rally themselves to perform these corporal mercies, why not society at large? "How," Crane asked, "is our country doing on these actions?"[6]

Writing from Danbury prison in 2021, activist Martha Hennessy commented on the quality of items allotted to inmates: "In the prison system no shoddy goods can be bad enough for the prisoners. Textiles that bleed dye and remain rough after washing, food that is raised by petrochemical means, pencils that are impossible to sharpen, clothing that stains and holds smells and wears out in a matter of weeks—the list is long. There is a tale in the Catholic Worker community of Dorothy [Day] sitting on a chair, it breaks and collapses, [and] she comments that now it is ready to donate to the poor."[7]

The abuse Rice noted early in the incarceration process when she and others were left shivering on a tarmac only increases the trauma of women who are then dumped into crowded prisons. Officials, many of whom are overworked and underpaid, can become petty, such as when they arbitrarily confiscated Rice's eyeglasses, even though reading is often one of the only substantive consolations for a prisoner. Reading with others is also an important means of education, providing basic literacy assistance for the many who cannot read or write well. To deny someone a pair of glasses is akin to deliberately keeping them uneducated, even though prison studies show a strong correlation between having an education and staying out of jail or prison.

In the Knox County jail, Rice observed certain officials continuously thinking up ways to "incriminate, punish, and suppress the most vulnerable citizens," she wrote in March of 2014.[8] She noted that she was accused of carrying "dangerous contraband" when a guard found a paperclip on one of her documents. The jail actually made money on prisoners' calls, billing long-distance calls at $1.35 per minute, making it difficult or impossible for poorer prisoners to connect with their families, which could have a powerful, negative impact on children, partners, and extended family.

When journalist Linda Stasi visited Rice, she was appalled at the conditions in Brooklyn's Metropolitan Detention Center.

> At 5 p.m., the official start of visiting hours, we were brought into a large, chilly room with armless chairs lined up in rows overseen by one guard. On one side was a sad "playroom" for the prisoners' children, perhaps 8-by-10 feet, with nothing but a few dirty stuffed animals.
>
> Visiting was supposed to be from 5 p.m. to 7:30 p.m., but it wasn't until 5:45 p.m. that prisoners were brought in.
>
> I recognized Sister Megan—she was the only 84-year-old woman. She also had a big smile, wide-spread arms, and a missing front tooth.[9]

Rice sometimes used her privilege as a nun, older woman, and educated advocate to push back on outrageous pettiness, for the sake of weaker prisoners who could not. One day she resisted an unnecessary strip search designed merely to humiliate her—the process for women involved removing all clothing, squatting down low in front of a guard, and coughing, to prove she didn't have anything illegal hidden in her body—feeling she did so on behalf of others. As Ellen Barfield says, "It is deeply disrespectful, and meant to be."[10]

John Amidon notes that these are elements of the prison system that many of unaware of. "There is no way to fully understand what it means to be a prisoner without having been one. First there is the processing before you are assigned a pod or cellblock. The loss of control, the humiliation, being commanded to strip naked . . . then squat and grunt in case you are attempting to carry items into jail . . . begins now. Given the differences of anatomy I can only imagine a woman's experience. A visitor or worker has little to none of this experience, a very different processing."[11]

Jerry Zawada told Rosalie Riegle of a strip search that turned into assault:

> Now many of the guards would just pretend to do that . . . that full search, but some were sticklers, and one day they called other guards, pushed me against the wall and ripped off my clothes, and they . . . and invaded my body. . . .
>
> I was put in solitary confinement for about ninety days and finally my security level was raised and I was shipped out. They call it "diesel therapy," when they send you from prison to prison around the country. To take you down. You're deprived of almost everything. It's harder to make a phone call, it's harder to take a shower, harder to get anything. Nobody knows where you are. They can hide you for a long time like that.[12]

For Rice's refusal, she got thirty-one days in lockdown, without phone calls, visits, or commissary. The latter may sound small, but it is an important part of daily mental health, in a world where little things become precious. Her niece Megan Tourlis recalls visiting along with son Tim Pettonlina and finding Rice eager for a treat from the vending machines where only outsiders were allowed to make purchases. Although Rice is a slim person who does not generally focus on food, small graces had become more important during this period of deprivation.

In prison, one normally does not ask fellow prisoners what they did to be incarcerated, but lockdown is different. Because it is a second step, it's part of normal conversation to find out how everyone got there, in part to be able to avoid such missteps in the future. When Rice asked other women what they did to be in lockdown, they spoke of minor infractions, such as "refusing" to get up when actually quite sick or saving an arthritis pain pill to help them sleep at night ("hoarding"). When a Knox County commissioner visited the jail, Rice was able to meet with her (thanks to privilege discussed in the next chapter) and she advocated for these others. Not enough changed, but at least those confiscated eyeglasses were all returned.

Activist Susan Crane reported similar practices around the same time at the federal prison in Dublin, California, a facility of about one thousand women: "Every day I saw women held in what I would call deliberate neglect, oppression, [with] victims of corruption and physical torture. There was no chance for redemption, forgiveness or reconciliation with the community. The prison is an institution of revenge and punishment."[13]

Crane pointed out a tragic dynamic. When nations or corporations commit war crimes or participate in environmental destruction, they do so with impunity, even though these actions are wholly unacceptable to society when individuals commit them. Worse, the national or corporate version does much more damage. "As a society we have decided that it's OK to bomb other countries, to use drones to kill other leaders, to kill children [when they are] in schools and at play. Yet individually we know that it's wrong to get a gun or a knife and murder our neighbors."[14] Society can spend half of every discretionary income tax dollar on nuclear weapons, she continued, but if a family spent that kind of money on weapons, people would be horrified.

Unlike Rice's experience of petty cruelty from officials and guards, however, Crane encountered better leadership in California. Calling it "an amazing contradiction," she cited how compassionate the staff and guards could be despite budget cuts, bureaucracy, and ongoing issues with their union. "There were people who kept their humanity and tried to be responsive to the needs of the women," although she was always cognizant of the fact that, "at the end of the day, if I climb the fence, they are willing to shoot me."[15]

Boertje-Obed found Leavenworth prison, with 1,600 inmates, to be the largest, most violent, and most racially segregated of the prisons in his protest experience. The guards were so unhappy that many had been picketing outside. They assigned him to a quiet block with older men, but he still knew of stabbings and of one man being beaten bloody and unconscious with a heavy lock. In an oral history with Rosalie Riegle, Jesuit Bill Bichsel said,

> What I remember especially about the LA County Jail was my first night. They dragged a man out of a cell and kicked the hell out of him. Women guards as well. I couldn't believe it! [At intake], they had us all strip and throw all our clothes into a big pile, and then they deloused us. With a spray hose.

They were really fooling around with it, getting a big kick out of where they hit [you] and stuff like that. All the guards carried big, rubber-headed flashlights. 'Flashlight therapy' they called it [because] they'd use it as a billy club.[16]

Inmates often scour the news for information about someone being sentenced to their facility, and they often "welcome" more notorious prisoners. Sometimes the welcome is violent and sometimes it is peaceful, depending on how those who are already incarcerated perceive the new inmate's crimes. The Y-12 action made a lot of news, so Boertje-Obed did have something of a welcoming committee, and he was fully aware that he might be in danger. However, he was fortunate. In a letter from prison published in *The Nuclear Resister*, he described a "host of angels" who helped him obtain little but precious things such as shower shoes and soap.[17]

"If you're nonviolent, God is with you," Boertje-Obed told author Michael Gallagher during the trial for Nuclear Navy Plowshares in May of 1988. "Dangerous situations sometimes occur. I've never been assaulted. I've felt the need to intervene when others were fighting, and things always worked out. You take the risk and you trust. You know that you're living with these guys, many of whom are in for murder and other serious crimes. But everybody has good in them. You take one day at a time, and you begin to feel more strongly that you have everybody as a brother. And you'll find that there are others who want to do the same thing and who are interested in talking about the Bible."[18]

Paul Magno also remembers that a surprising number of fellow inmates supported the activists. "It's always an open question how any other prisoners might react to your presence or your action. But one man in our jail sketched a man beating a sword into a plowshare and gave it to us as a gift. The image was of a very muscular Black man, like the artist himself, pounding away at an anvil."[19] Gallagher also writes about Magno, describing how he was even able to take advantage of lax Orange County jail security in Florida after Pershing Plowshares to use a pay phone and be a call-in guest for a radio talk show for an hour and a half. The freedom of the phone depended on the largesse of his fellow inmates, who "enjoyed having a celebrity in their midst." And of course white privilege was a factor.

White Privilege

> *One little, two little, three little white men,*
> *Four little, five little, six little white men,*
> *Seven little, eight little, nine little white men,*
> *Ten little white men, juror boys*
> *(And fo-ur women)*[20]

Activist Ralph Hutchison satirically improvised this song, to the tune of the old "Ten Little Indians" nursery rhyme, before a group of Transform Now Plowshares supporters when asked for a summary of the long, boring first day of jury selection at the Knoxville trial. Satire aside, the reality is that judges, juries, and criminal justice systems overall do skew white.

Plowshares activists have long understood that white privilege is a factor in how they are treated and how it is possible for some of them to commit similar actions multiple times while avoiding the harsher sentences that a person of color might receive.

Asked whether white privilege affected how she and others were treated in prison, Megan Rice answers confidently, "Well, surely!" She was able to observe first-hand differences in treatment between white, middle-class prisoners like herself and the poor women of color who made up the majority of the prison population.

Sue Frankel-Streit considers Plowshares actions a way for "white people of privilege to attempt to take some responsibility for warmaking." One thing that indicates for her the reality of white privilege in jail, she said,

> is that I wasn't really afraid ninety-nine percent of the time. I wasn't afraid I was going to be killed. So there's that at a basic level, [having] the support to be in a position to take those kinds of risks. . . .
>
> Rich, white, American Christians like charity, and I lived in a Catholic Worker house that was supported by people richer than we were. So we didn't have to work hard to have our needs met. We didn't come out of homelessness. We were healthy enough in mind and body [to weather incarceration]. We had a ton of support on the outside. And we may have had immunity, because of our support, to some of the direct effects of some of the scariest things that happen in there.

When asked if prison frightened her, she said no, but "it really unmasks the power structure in our society. And it was scary to see so many women living on the edge in a really depressed state. But I didn't fear for my own safety."[21]

Activist Jackie Allen-Douçot does remember being afraid during a situation that escalated before she realized what was happening when she refused to submit to a possibly invasive search.

> The captain or lieutenant or someone heard about this, and he dragged me to his office. I had these handcuff earrings on because I was young and kind of obnoxious, right? And he saw the earrings and he said, "Oh, you think this is a big joke." And he pushed me up against the wall. He said,

"What would you say if I told you I could have four men come in and hold you down?" I said, "I would say that makes you a rapist." [Then] the other officer came in and separated us and took me out. I ended up getting released the next day, but that was pretty scary and traumatizing.

[White privilege figures in because] the protesters are super well-connected, and they know that. We have good lawyers. We have lots of resources. They know that we're not poor people of color. And so we do have power and privilege that other people don't have. So I think that definitely gives a layer of protection. So while I was terrified when the guy was shoving me around, I also was pretty sure I would not be raped, because he knew that I was part of this bigger community and that he wouldn't be able to get away with it. And that's not a luxury that a lot of people of color have when they're in jail.[22]

English Ploughshares activist (note alternate spelling) Martin Newell said, "I know a track by [folk singer and labor organizer] Utah Phillips where he quotes [Catholic Worker and pacifist] Ammon Hennacy as telling him he was 'as a white man, born into mid-twentieth century industrial America, he was born with an arsenal of weapons, the weapons of privilege: racial privilege, sexual privilege, economic privilege.' The same would apply to someone like me born into suburban London, England."[23]

Kings Bay Plowshares 7 activist Clare Grady said, "As for observing white privilege in the protest, arrest, trial, sentencing stages . . . it is safe to assume that white privilege follows us white people around wherever we go, and that it functions in all the above."[24]

Des Moines Catholic Worker and activist Frank Cordaro adds, "The possession and intent to use our USA nuclear arsenal is the epitome of white privilege, though not limited to white privilege. It's also sexist and classist and every other -ism."[25]

Molly Rush of the original Plowshares Eight simply said, "I believe that everyone in the courtroom was white."[26]

Resilience

Michael Walli often wrote poetry in jail and prison, and some of it reflected the conditions around him. He wrote "Elevating the Host" in August of 2013, during his sentence for the Y-12 action. It reads in part,

> Without sacrifice there is no love
> Never forget that come what may
> Who does God's Work shall get God's pay
> Many saints have been squeezed into sanctity
> Thru the pinch of poverty[27]

At Leavenworth, Boertje-Obed felt some pressure to sit at certain tables for meals because he was white and Christian, since the men fairly strictly segregated themselves by race and religion. This was no small issue. A person could get beaten up to remind him not to sit at the wrong table. But white-people-only dynamics have always bothered Boertje-Obed, especially in church circles, and he prefers diversity. It took some time and observation to find a more integrated group where he could also sit safely, without being hassled by either inmates or guards. Even movies, recreation, and materials were divided by race, right down to the use of the iron to press their clothes: "There is a 'black iron,' " he wrote, "a 'white iron,' a 'Native American iron.' "[28] Some chaplains tried to address it, but to little avail. In the rare case that a white inmate and a black inmate would ever agree to share a cell, they could get beaten or receive death threats. And it wasn't just a black/white issue, for as Rice noted, prison brought together "Caribbean islanders, Russians, Koreans, Chinese, South and North Americans, Samoan and Thailanders, Israelis, and U.K. citizens and residents."[29]

Overcrowding generally makes the race issue, or any problem, worse. Rice was crammed in with over one hundred women in a space designed for pre-trial detainees, not long-term prisoners. It had originally been a men's high-rise detention facility, but as noted earlier, the women were moved in to free up their Danbury federal prison space for men crowded out of other prisons. The room was filled with bunks. Because it was designed for men who typically spend less time in the restroom, there were only six toilets for all of them and just one narrow, high window offering mere glimpses of the outside. As a lover of nature and science, one of Rice's challenges was having absolutely no outdoor space to walk in. Prison reformers have imagined thousands of creative alternatives to this common problem, but lack of money and will means that little changes over time.

Prison often sends people out worse than when they went in. Beyond the violence, there is also just a soul-crushing lack of resources. For example, Leavenworth used to have prison industries, including a furniture unit that even made some items for the White House, but all that closed for lack of funding.

Because of Boertje-Obed's desire to build community, he played Scrabble with inmates. He also tried to be useful to his cellmate, a Vietnamese man charged with arson that led to someone's death. Thanks to an inept public defender, the man endured a mistrial, and only after threatening suicide did he get a new lawyer, who then advised him to just plead guilty. That bad advice led to a life sentence, even though the prosecution didn't prove the arson. Whether he was guilty or not, he hadn't intended to kill anyone. Boertje-Obed was able to use both his literacy and his knowledge of judicial systems to help the man find a *pro bono* lawyer for an appeal. He was also able to empathize, which is in itself a gift to other prisoners. He shared an OREPA booklet with the man that included an apt quote: "One does not become compassionate without suffering."[30]

In years past, Tom Lewis and Phil Berrigan helped prisoners in the Baltimore County Jail write letters to their families and their judges. This gift of their literacy in the service of justice may have changed the outcome of some worthy cases for the better. Susan Crane became part of a suicide prevention program during her stay in federal prison.

Phil Berrigan wrote of his initial shock at the hardships of incarceration in *Fighting the Lamb's War*. The physical atmosphere was ugly and forbidding, but he also felt a deep satisfaction, that incarceration "makes the most sense."[31] Many activists mention this, describing a complex interplay between the grotesque deprivations of prison and the inner consolations of peace and purpose. Although no one reports liking prison, this rich spiritual sense of equanimity and even contentment is often a surprise for the new activists. It is a familiar, welcome sensation for those who have been incarcerated many times, returning like a trusted companion.

In a letter from the Metropolitan Detention Center in Brooklyn, Rice wrote this about the resilience of her fellow inmates: "One of my frequent thoughts is, 'My, how great these sister (or brother) inmates really are!' I guess, like people everywhere: so wise, so enduringly and endearingly patient, strong, creatively thoughtful and perceptive of often unexpressed wants or real needs of others."[32] This is not just a nun trying to cheer herself up. It is a way of reimagining the world daily, in any walk of life, and thus perceiving in reality what the mind can envision.

"There are wonderful people in prisons," she told a journalist after her initial incarceration prior to trial. "It was really hard for me to leave."[33] Some of the women inside, whom she loved very much and still writes to, gave her a track suit as a token of their affection, and she wore it for some of her media interviews. She doesn't associate being outside with freedom or being inside with loss of it, because she has interior freedom.

And it's not just Rice. You can sense this inner calm and groundedness in the presence of other Plowshares activists who have done time for peace. Jerry Zawada has recalled: "I feel it's my privilege to listen to them. People with very severe problems would come to me, sometimes in tears. There's a keen sense of abandonment [in prison], abandonment by families, abandonment by life. One guy said he wanted to be baptized Catholic, so I baptized him underneath the oak trees. If there was a way I could have stayed in, I would have done that. . . . I just miss the guys so much."[34]

Martha Hennessy wrote of the awkwardness and pain surrounding the contemplation of her own release: "[S]ome inmates have separated themselves from our interactions, as superficial as some may be. Relationships and sharing of daily life mean something to me, but the pain of some people being released while others are not is just too hard for some to bear, especially those here for more than a year or two."[35]

Serving, Teaching

In one of her letters from Danbury prison, Rice pointed out specific needs that she only could have understood by being on the inside. She wrote, "The need is urgent for local (retired) lawyers to be found who can assist inmates who need second opinions. The women need consultants they can trust, especially out-of-towners who have no connections in New York while imprisoned here away from young families for years pre-trial or pre-sentencing!"[36] She also encouraged supporters to join groups such as Families Against Mandatory Minimums.

Greg Boertje-Obed helped prisoners hone their methods to get things they needed. After he observed a hunger strike in a prison in Louisiana, he thought about how it could have been done more effectively. He helped organize the next one, showing prisoners how to type a list of reasonable demands, make copies, and distribute them so that strikers would all be on-message. As prisoners got better at organizing their strikes, sometimes they did get what they wanted. Nevertheless, as an organizer he was punished with time in solitary confinement (and yes, he says, some really do call it "the hole").

Is solitary confinement torture? Overall yes, but it also depends on who is going into the hole and why. Because Boertje-Obed had emotional support from the outside, was able to read and write, and knew how to pray, he was able to endure solitary. He explained that it is often possible to tap on the pipes or walls and communicate with other people, and that sometimes, due to prison overcrowding, "solitary" can actually be with another person, allowing a limited amount of ministry and sharing. Steve Kelly, SJ, often did long stretches in solitary confinement, and he tried to adapt it into a form of monastic practice.[37]

But it is a serious, even criminal, mistake to conclude from their experiences that solitary is ever an acceptable form of punishment. For a person without friends on the outside, who is unable to read and write in any meaningful way, and whose interior life may be racked with addiction, regret, guilt, fear, or the confusion of an unwell mind, solitary confinement is torture. Many poor people of color, particularly strong men whom prison guards may fear, receive sentences in solitary that add up to years and even decades, not just days or weeks.[38]

Michael Walli wrote from McKean federal prison in May of 2015 about solitary as torture: "The United States Constitution as originally written prohibited cruel and unusual treatments and punishments (and still does). If torture is not cruel and unusual treatment or punishment, what is? The World War I era US suffragette Alice Paul was unjustly arrested, jailed and force fed during her hunger strike as an inmate. The forced feeding of fasting/hunger striking prisoners has been defined to be a form of torture but it is still being used by the US government employees who operate the Guantanamo Bay concentration camp in eastern Cuba."[39]

* * *

While Boertje-Obed was in Leavenworth, wife Michele Naar-Obed and daughter Rachel waited for him. Naar-Obed was shocked when she and her daughter were asked to leave a Catholic Worker community house in Duluth, where they had been living, because it did not support Boertje-Obed's action. She wrote to *The Nuclear Resister* in July 2014 that "the timing couldn't have been worse."[40] Just as Naar-Obed began to despair, however, the wider Catholic Worker movement stepped in and supported her, along with Veterans For Peace and the Benedictine Sisters of St. Scholastica in Duluth. "The Sisters told us that this action is valued, it is needed, it is Spirit led and it is, in fact, pleasing in God's eye. When my Christian Peace Team in Iraqi Kurdistan found out about the witness, they embraced us and many of my Kurdish friends wrote letters of support during and after the trial. All of this validation helped me pour my life's energy back into the support of the action and back into following our vocation as individuals and family."[41]

Naar-Obed and their daughter joined the Hildegard Catholic Worker House, also in Duluth. During this time she had vivid dreams of Anne Montgomery, Elmer Maas, and Phil Berrigan. "All of them have let me know that they are with us on this journey." Now, instead of feeling rejected by the Catholic Worker, she could see that the sentiments were only in that one house. Overall she reported feeling embraced.

Tom Lewis and Phil Berrigan both commented on something that bothered Rice the most: many prisoners of color were doing long stretches of time for nonviolent crimes. For example, she became close with Michelle West, a woman serving two life sentences plus fifty years. Her crime was driving a car for men who were supposed to be doing a drug deal but who instead committed murder. One of the actual murderers got full immunity for turning in the others, including West. So the man killed someone and went free. Meanwhile West, who killed no one, did not plan to, and had no record, has now spent close to thirty years in prison. Rice has advocated for her ever since, using the celebrity surrounding her name to draw attention to unjust sentences for poor women of color. The National Association of Women Judges joined her in this effort. She also helped a Haitian immigrant who was facing deportation after her upcoming release; Rice referred her to Casa Cornelia, a San Diego law center founded by SHCJ sisters.

Rice also organized a daily prayer group that several women attended, and she started a book circle. This helped many women improve their reading and, in some cases, to read books for the very first time. Many of the activists consider tutoring and reading instruction to be a significant part of their ministry. Both Anne Montgomery and Ardeth Platte had long ministries helping prisoners prepare to take the GED.

Because of her decades of teaching experience in the United States and Africa, Rice entered prison with an expertise at connecting with adult learners. She drew on a teaching method promoted by Paulo Freire, author of *Pedagogy of the Oppressed,* a book that she used in Africa and has long been popular with activists who teach in poor communities. She said his method was effective in teaching adults to read in as little as six weeks.

Rice also used materials from the women-led Grailville in Loveland, Ohio, which offers teachers and civil servants an effective technique to relate to nonliterate adults and share literacy and religious education. "When people speak the things that are bugging them," she said, "the urgent issues of vocabulary come out. You help them put words on what they are trying to say, and then you save those words and you categorize them. These are the first words you teach. People are so willing and wanting to talk. It's a very exciting thing. It gets them to learn by articulating their injustices and the issues that bug them, or the things that please them. It gives them a voice."[42]

Another book she liked was *Training for Transformation: A Handbook for Community Workers,* by Anne Hope and Sally Timmel. She used elements of this methodology in both Nigeria and Ghana, so it was now a natural transition for her to engage it with women in prison. She said that in Africa, "we didn't start with doctrines, and dogmas, and catechism, and memorizing the Bible. We always started with personal experience of the adults. Then, in religious education we'd get into a biblical place or spot that exemplified the same situation and problem. Then finally, it was a synthesis where you decided what to do. It was certainly training for transformation. They were deciding themselves. Teenagers would be having conflict with a friend, or something, and they tried to do it in a way that it was not imposing. . . . It was sort of a leadership training too, really."[43]

She concluded, "You learn how to listen." Her listening may have been the first true, attentive, nonjudgmental ear many had ever experienced.

PLOWSHARES SACRAMENTS: WHITE ROSES

Among the objects carried onto the Y-12 grounds, the Transform Now Plowshares activists brought four white roses. When asked about it, Michael Walli offered a pamphlet on the White Rose student resistance movement against Hitler's Nazi regime.

In 1942, a small group of students formed the White Rose to oppose Nazi atrocities. Sophie and Hans Scholl, Alexander Schmorell, Willi Graf, and Christoph Probst were part of a circle around philosophy professor Kurt Huber at the University of Munich. Because most of them studied medicine, several went to the warfront and learned firsthand the horrors of war.

White Rose members all resigned from Hitler Youth, something everyone in Germany joined automatically as children. They distributed leaflets calling on workers to disrupt the arms industry. In a style we see in Plowshares today, they scrawled graffiti such as "Freedom" and "Hitler mass murder" on the city hall and other buildings. They started groups to read and circulate banned books, such as works of philosophy and religion. According to the US Holocaust Memorial Museum, they sent messages such as "We will not be silent," and "We are your bad conscience" to their fellow students. "The White Rose will not leave you in peace!"

The Gestapo captured them in 1943. After show trials, the Scholls and Probst were convicted and executed by guillotine, with Kurt Huber tried and executed later.[44]

A Plowshares action called the White Rose Disarmament took place on June 2, 1987. Katya Komisaruk, a peace activist from the San Francisco Bay area, walked through an unlocked gate at the NAVSTAR satellite control facility at the Vandenberg Air Force Base in Santa Barbara County, California. The facility was home to an early global positioning system that used eighteen orbiting satellites to navigate the Trident II and other nuclear missiles, as well as the 1980s "Star Wars" nuclear attack system, for a first-strike nuclear attack. She damaged equipment and spray-painted "NUREMBERG" and "INTERNATIONAL LAW," along with disarmament slogans.[45]

Komisaruk gave the Mrs. Fields Cookies brand brief notoriety because she left a box of them, along with flowers and a poem. There was even a Miss Manners column about it ("What does a lady wear to her first felony trial?"),[46] *but it was not humorous for Komisaruk. After prison she entered Harvard Law School and became a civil rights lawyer.*

CHAPTER TWELVE

You Can Jail the Resisters but Not the Resistance

None of the trio in Transform Now Plowshares served their full sentences. On Tuesday, May 8, 2015, after two years of incarceration, they won their appeal of the most serious charge for which they were convicted, sabotage.

Not Saboteurs

The opinion from a three-judge panel of the Sixth Circuit Court of Appeals, with one dissent, is remarkably direct.

> The defendants' actions in this case had zero effect, at the time of their actions or anytime afterwards, on the nation's ability to wage war or defend against attack. Those actions were wrongful, to be sure, and the defendants have convictions for destruction of government property as a result of them. But the government did not prove the defendants guilty of sabotage.
>
> That is not to say, of course, that there is nothing a defendant could do at Y-12 that would violate § 2155(a). If

a defendant blew up a building used to manufacture components for nuclear weapons, for example, and thereby prevented the timely replacement of weapons in the nation's arsenal, the government surely could demonstrate an adverse effect on the nation's ability to attack or defend—and, more to the point, that the defendant knew that his actions were practically certain to have that effect. But vague platitudes about a facility's "crucial role in the national defense" are not enough to convict a defendant of sabotage. And that, in the last analysis, is all the government offers here.

The question, then, is whether the defendants consciously meant to interfere with the nation's ability to attack or defend when they engaged in those actions. No rational jury could find that the defendants had that intent when they cut the fences; they did not cut them to allow al Qaeda to slip in behind.[1]

In another bracing turn of phrase, the opinion from Judge Raymond Kethledge (who happened later to also become a Republican short-lister for potentially open US Supreme Court seats, just as Judge Amul Thapar would be) read, "First Amendment issues aside, it takes more than bad publicity to injure the national defense."[2] And thus one deeply conservative judge wrote the majority opinion overturning the ruling of another one, and Plowshares scored a victory, making it difficult in the future for another court to make the charge of sabotage stick.

Ralph Hutchison noted with delight in an OREPA press release, "They were nonviolent protesters in the tradition of Gandhi, not saboteurs. We are pleased the Sixth Circuit appreciated the difference."[3] It was, in the words of Sr. Ardeth Platte, "a great win for Plowshares in the higher court."[4] However, John LaForge added this sobering observation,

"What remains unscathed is the White House's plan to spend $1 trillion on new weapons production facilities over the next 30 years—$35 billion a year for 3 decades. The role of the Highly Enriched Uranium Materials Facility in this Bomb production—a clear violation of the Nuclear Non-Proliferation Treaty—was named with blood by the Plowshares action, but the H-bomb business marches on."[5]

Only the destruction of government property ("depredation" in government-speak) convictions remained, and they had served their time on those. They were still ordered to pay $52,000 in fines, but Catholic sisters and priests are usually not required to do this, as the government acknowledges their indigence because of the vow of poverty, in what can be considered yet another instance of privilege. Since Boertje-Obed and Walli both live under the minimum income requirements for filing income tax, in order to keep from providing financial support to US weaponry systems, the fine was merely symbolic. They did run the risk of a rehearing if the government demanded one, but that didn't happen.

The reversal was an interesting dogleg in Judge Amul Thapar's bright and rising career. Edith Roberts, who was once the Supreme Court editor of the *Harvard Law Review* and clerked for Ruth Bader Ginsburg before Ginsburg was on the high court, analyzed Thapar's career for SCOTUSblog. She called *USA v. Walli* Thapar's best-known case to date and perhaps his most complex. Analyzing his reasoning that because the Constitution didn't give him a way to sentence peace protesters differently than terrorists, then he had no choice but to treat them the same, Roberts wrote, "Thapar denied their motion for a judgment of acquittal on the sabotage charge, reasoning that the Constitution leaves the judgment of whether 'it make[s] sense to deal as harshly with non-violent protesters as with foreign saboteurs' to the policymaking branches, so the Court must interpret this criminal statute by its terms."[6]

In others words, Thapar handed down a to-the-letter decision based on his originalist and textualist principles, yet it ultimately didn't fit the crime. The judge's post-sentencing comments also seemed to suggest that he thought a long stretch in prison might be somehow remedial, to mysteriously "bring them back to the political system I fear they have given up on."[7] This was a peculiar thing to say given that prison has never had that effect on any Plowshares activist, or arguably on any prisoner, ever. In fact, if anything could have possibly been designed specifically to make a person distrust the US political machine and rage against it mightily, it would be our broken and neglected prison system.

Rice learned she was getting out of the Metropolitan Detention Center in Brooklyn by hearing it on the BBC News. Cousin Megan Tourlis, who was visiting her that day, remembers an officer came into the visiting room to inform her that Rice would be released that afternoon. Rice had less notice than she did. Tourlis waited at the back gate for several hours, eventually joined by *Washington Post* reporter Dan Zak. Although a different prison official handled the release, Tourlis's son Tim Pettolina had a childhood friend who was a corrections officer, and he offered to carefully escort her out, thus making sure she was always in good hands.

In prison in McKean, Pennsylvania, Michael Walli heard the news in a phone call from one of their lawyers. A local Catholic priest came to meet him, and for a special reason. The priest had served time in the same facility for his protests against the Iraq war.

Greg Boertje-Obed actually thought he was in trouble when a guard called him in, and it was jolting emotionally. But the guard handed him the phone so his wife Michele could inform him. Then guards abruptly hustled him out with his few things and gave him a one-way bus ticket from Leavenworth, Kansas, to Knoxville, Tennessee. Just as no one in the prison system had ever made the least effort to have Boertje-Obed serve his sentence near his family in Duluth, so now no one helped him return home afterward (indeed, they gave him a ticket for a bus going in the wrong direction). One of the local Knoxville families who supported MGM during their action and trial showed what Ralph Hutchison called "the best of Southern hospitality" by inviting Boertje-Obed to stay overnight. Then, working with OREPA activists, the family arranged a ride for him back to Duluth.

This casual disregard for a prisoner's personal logistics leaves many poorer people unable to visit with their loved ones during incarceration or to readily return home after release. Even if one claims no personal sympathy for the prisoners themselves, what about their parents? Their children? Their partners? Such institutional indifference fractures families and divides communities.

By not giving any of the activists warning, the system also separated all three of them from prisoners they had befriended without an opportunity to say goodbye or have some closure on what had become close relationships. Rice stayed with her cousin Megan Tourlis until August, during which time Tourlis observed her "mourning and missing her fellow inmates" quite deeply.[8] She wore the same sweatpants and croc shoes that she wore in prison for several weeks, in solidarity. Tim Pettolina noted that she was very thin. The prison machine had no interest in her emotional needs or those of any of the prisoners. The case was over, and the system that had fought to keep the three of them now just wanted them gone.

Forward

Any time Rice travels these days, she has the dubious honor of seeing the letters *SSSS* emblazoned on her boarding pass, as do other Plowshares activists. This stands for "Secondary Security Screening Selection," and it means at the very least that she'll be pulled out of line to answer many questions. Sometimes airline employees pat her down. Occasionally she has to endure two pat-downs that can be rudely invasive. Even though she completed twenty-four months of what the parole system calls "unsupervised supervision" (whatever that means) and was supposed to have had the SSSS restriction removed after that, it never went away, thanks to bureaucratic red tape.

Rice lived in Washington, DC, for the first five years after her release, sharing a Holy Child community house in the Brookland neighborhood near Catholic University. This area has long been known as "Little Rome," because it includes houses—in some cases monasteries, in others smaller residences—of many Catholic congregations, including Franciscans, Dominicans, Josephites, Benedictines, and others on its tree-lined streets. Rice prayed daily with a group at the Assisi Community, a house founded by Marie Dennis and Joseph Nangle, OFM, that included Sr. Dianna Ortiz, OSU, a torture survivor, until her death from cancer in February 2021. Rice also remained quite active in the Dorothy Day Catholic Worker community, often taking the city bus that went almost directly from her door to theirs, a thirty-minute ride. Because Tim Pettolina is the house manager for the Broadway play *Hamilton*, she saw it three times, including once in dress rehearsal with Megan Tourlis. She loved the show. Pettolina gave her a backstage tour, and she met many members of the cast.

When the former Sacred Heart superior general Clare Pratt moved to the nearby Sacred Heart community named Anne Montgomery House, she and Rice became good friends. They got together with a mutual friend (the author) at least once a month for lunch and conversation about their shared interests. Conversations covered who was in prison now for Plowshares—they were both active in writing to prisoners—and how other peaceful civil resistance actions were going. In 2020, shortly after her ninetieth birthday, Rice moved to the Holy Child Community in Rosemont, Pennsylvania. When the 2020–21 pandemic finally relented, Pratt and the author continued to visit her at least once a month.

Michael Walli lives at the Dorothy Day Catholic Worker House on Rock Creek Church Road in Washington, DC. Although he participates in many protests, including some public appearances for Plowshares, he does not use a computer or cell phone, nor does he travel, so many of the post-prison restrictions do not affect him, although FBI agents have occasionally visited the house to ask him questions. He is a dedicated gardener, and it was heartwarming to see him helping Rice and her SHCJ sisters by digging vigorously in their Brookland garden before Rice moved to Rosemont. In his courtroom testimony he even called himself "a garlic farmer," as he is quite pleased with how well it grows for him in DC.

Greg Boertje-Obed returned to daily life at the Duluth Catholic Worker. Although he follows Plowshares news, he has other causes these days. "When I go to work or I volunteer at a soup kitchen or a homeless center," he says, "nobody's really talking about nuclear weapons. There are so many other issues. In our area, right now, it's an oil pipeline. The Native people . . . see that as a threat to the land, water, to their life, and they're doing a campaign."[9]

He and his wife Michele organized a pipeline resistance retreat at Standing Rock. White privilege was again a factor, as they used their ability to be treated differently than Native people by federal marshals in order to draw attention to the problem.

All three closely follow the news about the Kings Bay Plowshares 7, who entered the Kings Bay Naval Submarine Base in April 2018, and they know and write to all of the activists. To Greg Boertje-Obed, however, the only way to measure progress in Plowshares circles would be if the world saw some real, structural change. He encourages, for example, more nuanced dialogue about differences among capitalism, socialism, and other -isms, "so that there isn't this big gap in income and well-being. We're hoping that the poor would do better. The weapons are a factor in that, because we spend so much money on them, and it shows that our values are not for helping the poor in our country, or around the world."[10]

Steve Kelly, SJ, offered these words to those considering what to do about the proliferation of nuclear weapons.

> Plowshares is really an embodiment of that Biblical vision of conversion, and it's meant to wake up the sleeping giant. People of faith woke up in the previous century and abolished slavery, which was an institution that was around for thousands of years. People would say it was an economic necessity. . . .
>
> It's certainly a challenge for any of us to ask ourselves, well what am I doing for peace? Am I asleep? Or, God forbid, am I benefiting from the status quo? . . . Gandhi would say, whatever it is, ecologically, politically, do something. The nukes will be here to stay. They're not going away by themselves unless people take them on, repent of the building of them and production of them. . . . Unless

we address this pact to kill all life on earth, nothing really gets addressed. . . .

If anyone is active and committed, we'll probably meet up somehow or another, either in a court or a prison or even on the streets.[11]

We conclude with excerpts from a joint letter the three Transform Now Plowshares activists wrote on the second anniversary of their Y-12 action, compiled by Megan Rice.

Our "crime" was to draw attention to the criminality of the 70-year-old nuclear industry itself and to the unconscionable fact that the United States spends more on nuclear weapons than on education, health, transportation, and disaster relief combined. . . .

[O]ur action at Oak Ridge was based on the commonsense reality that we human beings have endured more than enough destruction and exploitation. We believe that we citizens can exercise our collective power to consciously transform our nation's priorities. We all need to actively insist on more humane uses for the billions of dollars now budgeted for the nuclear weapons/industrial complex.

Two years ago, as we neared the building in Oak Ridge, we were extremely surprised by the ineffectiveness of the system that supposedly guarded our nation's most important National Security Complex. We believed that we were about to expose the source of unfettered violence that has led to the chronic spiritual and economic decline in the US. As it turned out, it was the laxity of the security system at Y-12 that caught the attention of the courts and the mainstream media. Security weakness became the big story. There was no mainstream acknowledgement that the national security complex is rotting from its own irrelevance. . . .

In order for the US to negotiate for nuclear disarmament in good faith, we say it is essential to peaceably transform these very corporations so that they are no longer able to violate the most basic moral and legal principles of civilized society by deliberately precipitating planetary self-destruction.[12]

This book ends as it began, with the inevitability that these three life stories alone, or the narratives of any of these Plowshares activists, won't give historians that satisfying "why" we so often desire. So instead let us return to that pair of prophetic Scripture passages embraced by so many global faiths, whether Christians or Jews, Muslims or Mormons: Isaiah 2:4 and Micah 4:3. If one accepts biblical prophecy, then somehow swords must eventually turn into plowshares and spears into pruning hooks. Thus it is worth asking again, with gratitude for the faithful work of all of these activists who have done and will do time for peace.

If not nuclear weapons, what?
If not now, when?
And if not us, who?

War no more.

Take Action

https://nunspriestsbombsthefilm.com/
https://www.globalzero.org/
https://www.wagingpeace.org/nuclearzero/
https://famm.org/
https://nsquare.org/

Notes

Dedication—page v

1. Loring Wirbel, "Nukewatch-NR - Plowshares Eight Part 2," July 4, 2010, https://youtu.be/CcgdgWKwg4Q.

Preface—pages xiv–xviii

1. Dan Zak, *Almighty: Courage, Resistance, and Existential Peril in the Nuclear Age* (New York: Blue Rider Press, 2016).

2. Ardeth Platte, OP, and Carol Gilbert, OP, interview with the author, September 19, 2017.

3. Proposition One Campaign, "Charlie King sings to Transform Now! Plowshares, Knoxville TN, 5/6/13," https://youtu.be/Zu2rbbMq0ME. Magno's comments start at 13:21.

4. John LaForge, "Sabotage Conviction Overturned, new sentence ordered for Transform Now Plowshares," *The Nuclear Resister*, May 8, 2015.

5. Mark Rahner, "Old-vs-navy," *The Seattle Times*, April 12, 2010, https://youtu.be/63B_PaQatco.

6. Katie Rutter, "An Interview with Sr. Megan Rice," *St. Anthony Messenger*, December 26, 2018; Josh Harkenson, "This Guy Died and Asked For His Blood to Be Splashed on a Nuclear Facility," *Mother Jones*, January 16, 2014; Congressman Joe Barton (R-Texas) in "DOE's Nuclear Weapons Complex: Challenges to Safety, Security, and Taxpayer Stewardship," US Congress, House of Representatives,

Committee on Energy and Commerce, Subcommittee on Oversight and Investigations, Serial No. 112-175, September 12, 2012, 7.

7. Frank Munger, "A Year after Break-in, Y-12 Searches for Its Lost Reputation," *Knoxville News-Sentinel*, July 27, 2013, http://archive.knoxnews.com/news/local/a-year-after-break-in-y-12-searches-for-its-lost-reputation-ep-357911079-355625921.html/.

8. Nicholas Kristof, "Opinion: Sister Acts," *The New York Times*, August 16, 2014; Michael Edwards, "An Unexpected Cloud of Witnesses: Sister Rice Replies," *openDemocracy*, October 29, 2014.

9. HLN Headline News, "$53,000 for Sister's Act," WAE-TV, January 28, 2014, https://youtu.be/ubTYjUdZG1g.

10. Ardeth Platte, OP, email to the author, September 26, 2020.

Plowshares Sacraments—pages xxiii–xxiv

1. Ardeth Platte, OP, interview with the author, September 19, 2017.

2. Art Laffin, email to the author, October 6, 2020.

3. Megan Rice, SHCJ, interview with the author, August 18, 2018.

4. Daniel Berrigan, *Portraits of Those I Love* (New York: Crossroad, 1982), 131. Thank you to Fr. John Dear for suggesting the book.

5. Bill Frankel-Streit, interview with the author, November 2, 2020.

Chapter One—pages 1–21

1. Rice, interview with the author, November 29, 2019.

2. Madeleine Hooke Rice, *American Catholic Opinion in the Slavery Controversy*, Studies in History, Economics, and Public Law, 508 (New York: Columbia University Press, 1944).

3. Rice, interview with the author, December 29, 2018.

4. Frederick W. Rice, Entry in Archives and Special Collections, Augustus C. Long Health Sciences Library, Columbia University, https://www.library-archives.cumc.columbia.edu/obit/frederick-w-rice.

5. Frederick W. Rice, "Regarding Recent Efforts to Reduce Mortality in Childbirth," *American Journal of Obstetrics and Gynecology* 4, no. 3 (September 1922). See also "Frederick W. Rice," *Columbia Alumni News* 39 (May 1948): 32.

6. Rice, interview with the author, September 19, 2017.

7. Morningside Area Alliance, "Academic Acropolis," https://morningside-alliance.org/tour/academic-acropolis/.

8. Rice, interview with the author, February 14, 2018.

9. Rice, interview with the author, July 16, 2017.

10. Rice, interview with the author, July 16, 2017.

11. Rice, interview with the author, June 25, 2017.

12. Rice, interview with the author, October 10, 2019.

13. Statement of Disarm Now Plowshares, November 2, 2009, reprinted at http://www.jonahhouse.org/archive/Disarm_Now_Plowshares/statement.htm.

14. Kathy Kelly, email to the author, January 18, 2021.

15. United States Census Bureau, *Statistical Abstract of the United States*, "Education," June 1957.

16. Dan Zak, *Almighty: Courage, Resistance, and Existential Peril in the Nuclear Age* (New York: Blue Rider Press, 2016), 46.

17. Pat McSweeney, email with the author, April 24, 2021.

18. Rice, in "Swords into Plowshares Sr Megan Rice," May 7, 2013, https://youtu.be/SnqECJ9qPx4. The quote is one she uses often.

19. Rice, interview with the author, July 16, 2017.

20. Lydia Essien, email with the author, September 3, 2020.

21. Rice, interview with the author, February 14, 2018.

22. See Paulo Freire, *Pedagogy of the Oppressed*, 50th Anniversary Edition, trans. Myra Bergman Ramos (New York: Bloomsbury, 2018).

23. Rice, interview with the author, June 20, 2018.

24. Rice, interview with the author, February 14, 2018.

25. Rice, interview with the author, July 4, 2018.

26. Rice, interview with the author, July 4, 2018.

27. Rice, interview with the author, February 14, 2018.

28. Rice, interview with the author, January 27, 2018.

29. John LaForge, "Nuclear Weapons Protesters' Sabotage Conviction Overturned," *The Nuclear Resister*, May 12, 2015.

30. Martha Hennessy, "Reflections from Danbury," *The Nuclear Resister,* April 20, 2021.

Chapter Two—pages 22–39

1. United States District Court, Eastern District of Tennessee at Knoxville. *United States of America v. Walli et al.*, CR 12-107, Trial Day 2 of 3, May 7, 2013, 255. (Hereafter, this case will be referred to as *USA v. Walli et al.*, followed by reference to trial day/date and transcript page number. All trial transcripts are available at the Transform Now Plowshares blog, https://transformnowplowshares.wordpress.com/legal-arguments.)

2. Chief Johnnie Bobb, interview with the author, May 24, 2021.

3. John Amidon, email to the author, February 9, 2021.

4. For a history of the Western Shoshone claims, see John D. O'Connell, "Constructive Conquest in the Courts: A Legal History of the Western Shoshone Lands Struggle—1861 to 1991," *Natural Resources Journal* 42:4 (Fall 2002): 765–799. Also, Barbara McDonald, "How a Nineteenth Century Indian Treaty Stopped a Twenty-First Century Megabomb," *Nevada Law Journal* 9:3 (2009), https://scholars.law.unlv.edu/nlj/vol9/iss3/9.

5. Ryan Hall, email to the author, May 4, 2021.

6. COA News, "Interview with Father Louis Vitale," https://youtu.be/xZYSlANqtZw. He also tells the story in Other Voices, Other Choices, "Father Louis Vitale: Love Your Enemies," https://youtu.be/EB9LsuyZl9c.

7. Rosalie G. Riegle, *Crossing the Line: Nonviolent Resisters Speak Out for Peace* (Eugene, OR: Wipf and Stock, 2013), 320.

8. Other Voices, Other Choices, "Father Louis Vitale: Love Your Enemies."

9. Riegle, *Crossing the Line*, 320–21.

10. Br. Javier Del Ángel De Los Santos, OFM, 2015 video. Franciscan Interprovincial Novitiate, Burlington, Wisconsin. Part of the Facebook page, "Memories of Fr. Jerry Zawada, OFM," https://www.facebook.com/javierofm/videos/1273220249470434. Used with permission. The comment is at 7:00.

11. Brian Roewe, "Jerry Zawada, quiet, powerful presence in peace movement, dies," *National Catholic Reporter*, July 27, 2017.

12. Suzanne Becker, "Interview with Jerome Zawada," *Nevada Test Site Oral History Project*, August 9, 2006, https://cdm17304.contentdm.oclc.org/digital/collection/nts/id/1083.

13. Becker, "Interview with Jerome Zawada."

14. Riegle, *Crossing the Line*, 315.

15. De los Santos video.

16. Riegle, *Crossing the Line*, 317.

17. ASEP, "Sacred Peace Walk - Jerry Zawada - Eucharist," April 24, 2011, https://youtu.be/lh9xw_f9xdk.

18. Nevada Desert Experience, "Sister Megan Rice & Father Jerry Zawada at Creech AFB prior to arrests," September 17, 2020, https://youtu.be/N4ee-7kOfWc.

19. Peter Ediger, "A 'Mennonite Franciscan' Speaks," Franciscans for Justice, August 23, 2011, https://www.franciscansforjustice.org/2011/08/23/a-mennonite-franciscan-speaks.

20. Ediger, "A 'Mennonite Franciscan' Speaks."

21. For a video of Peter Ediger singing, see https://youtu.be/oo_TKAK1Nv8.

22. Julia Occhiogrosso, interview with the author, May 6, 2021; Ediger, "A 'Mennonite Franciscan' Speaks."

23. Congressman John Lewis, *Congressional Record*, House, September 30, 1993, page 23136. Seen in "Father Roy: Inside the School of the Assassins," https://youtu.be/DJhg_ZhU1xc. John Lewis (D-GA) is at 00:42.

24. Pablo Ruiz, "The 1989 University of Central America Massacre," School of the Americas Watch, March 17, 2019.

25. Roy Bourgeois, telephone interview with the author, February 10, 2021.

26. James Hodge and Linda Cooper, *Disturbing the Peace: The Story of Roy Bourgeois and the Movement to Close the School of the Americas* (Maryknoll: Orbis, 2004), 59.

27. Arthur Laffin, email to the author, January 20, 2021.

28. *USA v. Walli et al.*, Trial Day 3 of 3, May 8, 2013, 114.

29. Rosalie Riegle, *Voices from the Catholic Worker* (Philadelphia: Temple University Press, 1993), 43.

30. Kristen Tobey, *Swords into Plowshares: Nonviolent Direct Action for Disarmament* (New York: Harper & Row, 1987), 135.

31. Susan Crane, "Some Thoughts about Going onto Naval Base Kitsap/Bangor," Nov. 2, 2009, Jonah House website, http://www.jonahhouse.org/archive/Disarm_Now_Plowshares/cranestatement.htm.

32. Ralph Hutchison, "Detailed Account from Within the Trial of the Kings Bay Plowshares 7," Pressenza International Press Agency, October 25, 2019, https://www.pressenza.com/2019/10/detailed-account-from-within-the-trial-of-the-kings-bay-plowshares-7/.

33. Frances Crowe, "Friday Takeaway: Frances Crowe on Trying to Sink the U.S. Submarine Industry," *Daily Hampshire Gazette*, August 23, 2019.

Chapter Three—pages 40–58

1. Toward the end of her service in Africa, Rice often stayed there as she returned stateside more often to seek medical treatment for malaria and to spend time with her aging mother.

2. George Mische, "Inattention to Accuracy about 'Catonsville Nine' Distorts History," *National Catholic Reporter*, May 17, 2013.

3. Willa Bickham, email to the author, October 6, 2020; Brendan Walsh, email to the author, May 11, 2021; Jonathan Pitts, "Viva House Soup Kitchen Has Provided 45 Years of Service," *The Baltimore Sun*, April 14, 2013.

4. Garry Wills, *Outside Looking In: Adventures of an Observer* (New York: Viking, 2010), 60.

5. John Bach, interview with the author, April 27, 2021.

6. Jim Forest, *At Play in the Lions' Den: A Biography and Memoir of Daniel Berrigan* (Maryknoll, NY: Orbis, 2017), 334.

7. Mary Novak, interview with the author, September 19, 2017.

8. Carol Gilbert, OP, interview with the author, February 2, 2018.

9. Francis Boyle, *Protesting Power: War, Resistance, and Law*, War and Peace Library (Washington, DC: Rowman and Littlefield, 2007), 25.

10. Art Laffin, email to the author, October 14, 2020.

11. Mary Novak, interview with the author, September 12, 2017.

12. John Dear, *Peace Behind Bars: A Peacemaking Priest's Journal from Jail* (Franklin, WI: Sheed & Ward, 1995), 36.

13. Gregory Boertje-Obed, interview with the author, May 20, 2018.

14. *USA v. Walli et al.*, Trial Day 2 of 3, May 7, 2013, 214.

15. Paul Magno, interview with the author, June 3, 2020.

16. Philip Berrigan and Fred Wilcox, *Fighting the Lamb's War: Skirmishes with the American Empire* (Monroe, ME: Common Courage Press 1996), 96.

17. Berrigan and Wilcox, *Fighting the Lamb's War*, 20.

18. Berrigan and Wilcox, *Fighting the Lamb's War*, 79.

19. David Eberhardt, *For All the Saints: A Protest Primer* (David M. Eberhardt, 2020), 3–4; interview with author, June 5, 2021.

20. Berrigan and Wilcox, *Fighting the Lamb's War*, 79.

21. Richard T. McSorley, *My Path to Peace and Justice: An Autobiography* (Eugene, OR: Wipf and Stock, 1996), 119.

22. Paul Magno, email to the author, October 20, 2020.

23. Arthur Laffin and Anne Montgomery, RSCJ, *Swords into Plowshares: Nonviolent Direct Action for Disarmament* (New York: Harper & Row, 1987), 55, 65.

24. The following summary of Plowshares history draws on Art Laffin, "A History of the Plowshares Movement," *The Nuclear Resister,* October 22, 2019, https://www.nukeresister.org/2019/11/02/a-history-of-the-plowshares-movement-a-talk-by-art-laffin-october-22-2019/. Much of this section comes from his input.

25. Turin Film Corp, "Phillip Berrigan, Festival of Hope, Day 9, Part A," https://youtu.be/ZbqXoIbYC1M.

26. Daniel Sicken, interview with the author, May 25, 2020.

27. Frida Berrigan, *It Runs in the Family: On Being Raised by Radicals and Growing into Rebellious Motherhood* (New York: OR Books, 2015); Rosalie Riegle, *Doing Time for Peace: Resistance, Family, and Community* (Nashville: Vanderbilt University Press, 2012), 59.

28. Gregory Boertje-Obed, interview with the author, May 20, 2018.

29. Talking Stick TV, "Interview—Nonviolent Direct Action Against U.S. Nuclear Weapons Complex," November 28, 2010, https://youtu.be/xYDEfShO-zc.

30. Arthur Laffin, interview with the author, January 27, 2018.

31. Lynn Fredriksson, email to the author, October 5, 2020.

32. Rice, interview with the author, December 5, 2019. See KK Ottesen, ed., *Activist: Portraits of Courage* (San Francisco: Chronicle Books, 2019).

Chapter Four—pages 59–79

1. Anne Wachter, RSCJ, interview with the author, July 14, 2017.

2. Nancy Kehoe, RSCJ, interview with the author, July 14, 2017.

3. Virginia Dennehy, RSCJ, interview with the author, July 14, 2017.

4. John Dear, "'Violence Ends Where Love Begins': A Conversation with Sr. Anne Montgomery," *The Nuclear Resister*, May 1, 2012, https://www.nukeresister.org/2012/08/28/anne-montgomery-rscj -presente.

5. Sergio Vasquez, interview with the author, July 14, 2017.

6. Raymond Hunthausen, "Faith and Disarmament," in George Weigel, *Tranquillitas Ordinis: The Present Failure and Future Promise of American Catholic Thought on War and Peace* (Oxford: Oxford University Press, 1987), 172; reprinted at the Disarm Now Plowshares website, https://disarmnowplowshares.wordpress.com/2011/03/23 /faith-and-disarmament/#more-2275.

7. Anne Montgomery, RSCJ, undated letter to students, Papers of Megan Rice, SHCJ.

8. Art Laffin, interview with the author, January 27, 2018.

9. Sergio Vasquez, interview with author, July 15, 2017.

10. Carolyn Osiek, RSCJ, email to the author, April 4, 2018.

11. Kathy Kelly, email to the author, January 20, 2021.

12. William F. Trimble, *Admiral John S. McCain and the Triumph of Naval Air Power* (Annapolis, MD: Naval Institute Press, 2019), 201.

13. Robert C. Ehrhart and Alfred F. Hurley, eds., *Air Power and Warfare: The Proceedings of the 8th Military History Symposium* (Washington, DC: Office of Air Force History, Headquarters USAF, and United States Air Force Academy, 1979), 193.

14. Blake Kremer, interview with the author, December 29, 2017.

15. John Amidon, email to the author, May 6, 2021.

16. E. B. Arnolds and N. F. Garland, "Defense of Necessity in Criminal Law: The Right to Choose the Lesser Evil," *Journal of Criminal Law and Criminology* 65, no. 3 (September 1974): 285–301, cited at the US Department of Justice website, https://www.ojp.gov /ncjrs/virtual-library/abstracts/defense-necessity-criminal-law-right -choose-lesser-evil.

17. John Schuchardt, email to the author, May 11, 2021.

18. Rice, interview with the author, July 16, 2017.

19. John W. O'Malley, "Introduction," in John Russell and John Atteberry, eds., *Ratio Studiorum: Jesuit Education, 1540–1773* (Chestnut Hill, MA: Boston College, 1999), 5.

20. Judith Garson, RSCJ, interview with the author, July 14, 2017.

21. Nancy Kehoe, RSCJ, interview with the author, July 14, 2017.

22. Clare Pratt, RSCJ, interview with the author, January 2021.

23. Judith Garson, RSCJ, interview with the author, July 14, 2017.

24. Statement provided by Archivist Carolyn Osiek, RSCJ, and Associate Archivist Michael Pera, confirmed by Kathleen Conan, RSCJ, Paula Toner, RSCJ, and Clare Pratt, RSCJ, email with the author, July 19, 2021.

25. Dear, "'Violence Ends Where Love Begins.'"

26. Judith Garson, RSCJ, interview with the author, July 14, 2017.

27. Patrick O'Neill, "Triduum 2021," *The Nuclear Resister*, April 24, 2021, https://www.nukeresister.org/2021/04/24/from-fci-elkton -triduum-2021-prison-reflections-by-patrick-oneill/.

28. Louis Vitale, "How Can I Cope?" *The Nuclear Resister*, February 25, 2010, http://www.nukeresister.org/2010/06/05/from-lompoc -by-fr-louie-vitale-ofm/.

29. John Dear, *Peace Behind Bars: A Peacemaking Priest's Journal from Jail* (Franklin, WI: Sheed & Ward, 1995), 15.

30. Dear, *Peace Behind Bars*, 49.

31. Anne Montgomery, RSCJ, letter to Megan Rice, April 3, 2011, Papers of Megan Rice, SHCJ.

32. Todd Kaplan, "Pershing Plowshares: An Allegiance to Serving Life," *The Orlando Sentinel*, May 3, 1986.

33. *United States v. Montgomery*, 772 F.2d 733; Patrick O'Neill, "30 Years Later, Nuclear Threat Gives Urgency to Plea for Peace," *The Orlando Sentinel*, April 20, 2014.

34. O'Neill, "30 Years Later."

35. Originally printed in John Dear, *Seeds of Nonviolence* (Baltimore: Fortkamp, 1992), 106.

36. Blake Kremer, email to the author, July 11, 2020.

37. Martin Luther King Jr., *Stride Toward Freedom: The Montgomery Story* (New York: Harper and Brothers, 1958), 220. Dr. King

spoke the words at the Montgomery, Alabama, victory rally, December 3, 1956.

38. Milo Yellow Hair, awards presentation for the Nuclear-Free Future Foundation, October 28, 2015, https://youtu.be/tEno-0EtcqI.

39. Anne Montgomery, RSCJ, undated letter to Megan Rice, 2011, papers of Megan Rice, SHCJ.

Chapter Five—pages 80–95

1. *USA v. Walli et al.*, Trial Day 3 of 3, May 8, 2013, 111.

2. Gregory Boertje-Obed, interview with the author, May 20, 2018. Unless otherwise noted, other quotes by Boertje-Obed in this chapter refer to the same interview.

3. Gregory Boertje-Obed, email to the author, May 17, 2021.

4. Gregory Boertje-Obed and Michele Naar-Obed, "From USP Leavenworth . . . with a Reflection from His Wife, Michele Naar-Obed," *The Nuclear Resister*, July 27, 2014, https://www.nukeresister .org/2014/07/27/from-usp-leavenworth-by-greg-boertje-obed-with -a-reflection-from-his-wife-michele-naar-obed/.

5. Dietrich Bonhoeffer, *The Cost of Discipleship*, trans. Reginald H. Fuller (London: SCM Press, 1959), 3–9.

6. Michael Gallagher, *Laws of Heaven: Catholic Activists Today* (New York: Houghton Mifflin Harcourt, 1992), 69.

7. Rice, interview with the author, October 10, 2019.

8. Michael Walli, interview with the author, January 23, 2018. Other quotes from Walli in this chapter are from this interview.

9. *USA v. Walli et al.*, Trial Day 3 of 3, May 8, 2013, 52.

10. *USA v. Walli et al.*, Trial Day 3 of 3, May 8, 2013, 46.

11. *USA v. Walli et al.*, Trial Day 3 of 3, May 8, 2013, 73.

12. *USA v. Walli et al.*, Trial Day 3 of 3, May 8, 2013, 47.

13. Richard T. McSorley, *It's a Sin to Build a Nuclear Weapon: The Collected Works on War and Christian Peacemaking of Richard Sorley* (Eugene, OR: Wipf and Stock, 1991).

14. Bill Quigley, "CONVICTIONS: The Trial of the Weapons of Mass Destruction Here Plowshares Clowns," Jonah House website, http://www.jonahhouse.org/archive/WMD%20Here%20Plowshares /Legal/TrialQuigley.htm.

15. Steve Kelly, SJ, personal interview with the author, December 13, 2017.

16. Christopher Spicer, interview with the author, August 17, 2021.

17. Ralph Hutchison, Resistance for a Nuclear-Free Future conference, Maryville College, July 3, 2010, posted by Loring Wirbel, https://youtu.be/rs9uWtZdTY4.

18. Gregory Boertje-Obed, "Jail Reflection from Transform Now Plowshares Activist Greg Boertje-Obed," *The Nuclear Resister*, September 2, 2012, http://www.nukeresister.org/2012/09/02/jail-reflection-from-transform-now-plowshares-activist-greg-boertje-obed/.

19. Jerrold M. Post and Lara K. Panis, "Crimes of Obedience," *Democracy and Security* 1, no. 1 (January–July 2005): 33–40; Associated Press, "J. Robert Elliott, 96; Judge Overturned My Lai Decision," *Boston Globe*, June 30, 2006.

Chapter Six—pages 96–106

1. Dan Zak, *Almighty: Courage, Resistance, and Existential Peril in the Nuclear Age* (New York: Blue Rider Press, 2016), 25. The timeline and details in this chapter come from interviews, Zak's research, Frank Munger's research at *The Knoxville News-Sentinel*, and prosecution and defense timelines.

2. Michael Walli, interview with the author, January 27, 2018.

3. Frida Berrigan, "How a Nun, a Vet, and a Housepainter Stood Up to the Threat of Nuclear Weapons," *The Nation*, August 31, 2016.

4. National Nuclear Security Administration, "Virtual Tour of HEUMF at Y-12," https://youtu.be/wgEvNc-qQ0M; see also the Y-12 facility website, https://www.y12.doe.gov.

5. National Nuclear Security Administration, "Virtual Tour of HEUMF at Y-12."

6. Megan Rice, on behalf of the Transform Now Plowshares, "Open Letter from the Brooklyn Metropolitan Detention Center," July 28, 2014, http://www.nukeresister.org/2014/07/28/from-brooklyn-metropolitan-detention-center-by-sr-megan-rice/.

7. Knoxville News-Sentinel, "An Inside Look at the Deteriorating Alpha-5 Building," https://youtu.be/9uJq9Uig7I8. Oak Ridge Office of Environmental Management, "Recovery Cleanup Project at Y-12

Leaves Alpha 5 with an Empty Feeling," https://www.energy.gov/orem /articles/recovery-cleanup-project-y-12-leaves-alpha-5-empty-feeling.

8. Arthur Laffin, interview with the author, January 27, 2018; Josh Harkinson, "This Guy Died and Asked for His Blood to Be Splashed on a Nuclear Facility," *Mother Jones*, January 16, 2014; Dan Zak, "The Prophets of Oak Ridge," *The Washington Post Magazine*, April 30, 2013.

9. Jamie Satterfield, "Priest Recommits Self to Injustice . . . Then Sent to Prison," *The Knoxville News-Sentinel*, September 13, 2011. (The comment by the priest referred to in the problematic title of the article was actually about committing himself to *resistance* to injustice.)

10. John Dear, *Peace Behind Bars: A Peacemaking Priest's Journal from Jail* (Franklin, WI: Sheed & Ward, 1995), 1.

11. Bill Frankel-Streit, interview with the author, July 8, 2020.

12. Zak, *Almighty*, 56.

13. Frank Munger, "B&W Touts Security Improvements at Y-12 since Break-in," *Knoxville News-Sentinel*, March 16, 2013.

14. Brook Silva-Braga, "The Nun Who Broke into a US Nuclear-weapons Facility," *Washington Post* video, April 30, 2013, https:// youtu.be/BprP6tRZ8mk.

15. Gregory Boertje-Obed, "Reflection from Blount County Jail," *The Nuclear Resister*, September 24, 2012.

16. Zak, *Almighty*, 115.

17. Zak, *Almighty*, 116.

18. *USA v. Walli et al.*, Trial Day 2 of 3, May 7, 2013, 182.

19. *USA v. Walli et al.*, Trial Day 2 of 3, May 7, 2013, 181.

20. Michael Patrick, "Kirk Garland Talks about Firing from Y-12 after Protesters Entered Facility," *Knoxville News-Sentinel* video, https://youtu.be/FLTWZx2YlO4.

21. *USA v. Walli et al.*, Trial Day 2 of 3, May 7, 2013, 144.

22. Ellen Barfield, "Two Years On, the Crime Remains the Same: To Honor the Transform Now Plowshares, We Must Continue the Work of Disarmament," *The Nuclear Resister*, July 28, 2014, https:// www.nukeresister.org/2014/07/28/two-years-on-the-crime-remains -the-same-to-honor-the-transform-now-plowshares-we-must-continue -the-work-of-disarmament/.

23. Gregory Boertje-Obed, email to the author, January 5, 2021.

24. Carol Gilbert, OP, email to the author, October 12, 2020.

25. Bill Frankel-Streit, interview with the author, July 8, 2020.

26. Bill Frankel-Streit, interview with the author, July 8, 2020.

Chapter Seven—pages 107–18

1. See, for example, Disarm Now Plowshares, "Hearts Open, Come Together," December 23, 2010, https://youtu.be/Rdvj9Mid718.

2. Leonard Eiger, "Tribute to Anne Montgomery," September 5, 2012, https://youtu.be/KU-G4jn_hoQ.

3. Ralph Hutchison, "Arraignment Proceedings: A Second Account," Transform Now Plowshares blog, https://transformnowplowshares .wordpress.com/2012/07/30/arraignment-proceedings-a-second -account/#more-82.

4. *Knoxville News-Sentinel*, "Y12 Protesters Arrive at Federal Court," August 9, 2012, https://youtu.be/4bAYZKLJiBQ.

5. *Knoxville News-Sentinel*, "Y12 Protester Greg Boertje-Obed Talks about His Cause," September 12, 2012, https://youtu.be/OcZID 3gnFEQ.

6. *USA v. Walli et al.*, Trial Day 3 of 3, May 8, 2013, 159.

7. DisarmNowPlowshares, "Going Pro Se (Lynne)," December 13, 2010, https://youtu.be/Z8PArKvwiqs.

8. DisarmNowPlowshares, "Going Pro Se (Susan, Bix)," December 13, 2010, https://youtu.be/gEg_Q03A9Do.

9. Hutchison, "Arraignment Proceedings."

10. Gregory Boertje-Obed, email to the author, April 24, 2021.

11. *USA v. Walli et al.*, Trial Day 2 of 3, May 7, 2013, 255.

12. Ralph Hutchison, "Felony Charges and Two Releases for Y-12 Plowshares Activists," Transform Now Plowshares blog, https:// transformnowplowshares.wordpress.com/2012/08/03/report-on -transform-now-plowshares-court-appearance-august-3-2012/.

13. Hutchison, "Felony Charges and Two Releases."

14. Ralph Hutchison et al., "Transform Now Plowshares Indicted on Three Counts," Transform Now Plowshares blog, https:// transformnowplowshares.wordpress.com/tag/michael-walli/.

15. Transform Now Plowshares, "'Know That We Walk with You, Susan'—from Greg Boertje-Obed, Mike Walli, and Sr. Megan Rice," August 22, 2012, https://transformnowplowshares.wordpress.com /2012/08/22/know-that-we-walk-with-you-susan-greg-boertje-obed -mike-walli-and-sr-megan-rice/.

16. Liane Ellison Norman, *Hammer of Justice: Molly Rush and the Plowshares Eight* (Pittsburgh: Pittsburgh Peace Institute, 1989), ix.

17. Ralph Hutchison et al., "Greg Boertje-Obed Released, Awaiting Y-12 Trial," Transform Now Plowshares blog, September 12, 2012, https://transformnowplowshares.wordpress.com/2012/09/12 /greg-boertje-obed-released-awaiting-y-12-trial/.

18. LEPOCO Peace Center, "Ramsey Clark Honors Daniel Berrigan," https://youtu.be/R0KszzuZuU4; Patrick O'Neill, "Happy Birthday, Father Dan," *IndyWeek*, July 19, 2006, https://indyweek .com/news/archives/happy-birthday-father-dan/.

19. John Huotari, "Former Attorney General Says Y-12 Work Unlawful, Nuclear Weapons Should Be Eliminated," *Oak Ridge Today*, April 23, 2013.

20. Patrick O'Neill, "Jury Finds Transform Now Plowshares Guilty; 3 Activists Jailed Till September 23 Sentencing," *The Nuclear Resister*, May 11, 2013.

Chapter Eight—pages 119–25

1. John Amidon, email to author, May 7, 2021.

2. Pazamidon, "Transform Now Plowshares Trial May 6, 2013," https://youtu.be/gA0_CTf0A6w.

3. Lissa McLeod, email to the author, February 17, 2021.

4. Pazamidon, "Transform Now Plowshares Trial May 6, 2013."

5. *Knoxville News-Sentinel*, "Songs, Prayer Vigil for Y-12 Trio," May 9, 2013, https://youtu.be/iZ29aiAy8Ik.

6. Berrigan and Wilcox, *Fighting the Lamb's War: Skirmishes with the American Empire* (Monroe, ME: Common Courage Press, 1996), 90.

7. Rosalie G. Riegle, *Crossing the Line: Nonviolent Resisters Speak Out for Peace* (Eugene, OR: Wipf and Stock, 2013), 315.

8. Drew Christiansen, SJ, "Introduction," in Christiansen and Carole Sargent, eds., *A World Free from Nuclear Weapons: The Vatican Conference on Disarmament* (Washington, DC: Georgetown University Press, 2020).

9. John Amidon, email to the author, May 5, 2021.

10. John Amidon, email to the author, May 5, 2021.

11. Pope Francis, "Address to Participants in the International Symposium, 'Prospects for a World Free of Nuclear Weapons and for Integral Disarmament,'" November 10, 2017, https://www.vatican.va/content/francesco/en/speeches/2017/november/documents/papa-francesco_20171110_convegno-disarmointegrale.html.

12. Gregory Boertje-Obed, interview with the author, May 20, 2018.

13. Dan Zak, *Almighty: Courage, Resistance, and Existential Peril in the Nuclear Age* (New York: Blue Rider Press, 2016), 204.

Chapter Nine—pages 126–50

1. *USA v. Walli et al.*, Trial Day 2 of 3, May 7, 2013, 304–5.

2. *USA v. Walli et al.*, Trial Day 3 of 3, May 8, 2013, 5.

3. Andrew Wolfson, "Ky Judge on Short List for High Court," *Courier Journal*, December 9, 2016.

4. Melodi Erdogan and Jennifer Brake, "Elderly Nun Sentenced to Nearly 3 Years for Tennessee Nuclear Break-in," Reuters, February 18, 2014.

5. Kevin Allen, "Judge Amul Thapar Talks about Scalia and Religious Liberty," University of Notre Dame Law School, April 3, 2019, https://law.nd.edu/news-events/news/judge-amul-thapar-talks-about-scalia-and-religious-liberty/.

6. Oak Ridge Environmental Peace Alliance, "Day Two: Transform Now Plowshares Trial," https://orepa.org/day-two-transform-now-plowshares-trial.

7. *USA v. Walli et al.*, Trial Day 2 of 3, May 7, 2013, 24.

8. *USA v. Walli et al.*, Trial Day 2 of 3, May 7, 2013, 45.

9. Oak Ridge Environmental Peace Alliance, "Day Two: Transform Now Plowshares Trial."

10. *USA v. Walli et al.*, Trial Day 2 of 3, May 7, 2013, 145.

11. John Amidon, email to the author, May 7, 2021.

12. *USA v. Walli et al.*, Trial Day 2 of 3, May 7, 2013, 168.

13. *USA v. Walli et al.*, Trial Day 2 of 3, May 7, 2013, 206.

14. Ralph Hutchison, email to the author, May 12, 2021.

15. *USA v. Walli et al.*, Trial Day 2 of 3, May 7, 2013, 226.

16. *USA v. Walli et al.*, Trial Day 2 of 3, May 7, 2013, 234.

17. Barbara Bartlett, SHCJ, email to the author, April 20, 2021.

18. *USA v. Walli et al.*, Trial Day 2 of 3, May 7, 2013, 244.

19. *USA v. Walli et al.*, Trial Day 2 of 3, May 7, 2013, 257.

20. *USA v. Walli et al.*, Trial Day 2 of 3, May 7, 2013, 269.

21. *USA v. Walli et al.*, Trial Day 2 of 3, May 7, 2013, 271.

22. *USA v. Walli et al.*, Trial Day 2 of 3, May 7, 2013, 278.

23. *USA v. Walli et al.*, Trial Day 2 of 3, May 7, 2013, 278–79.

24. *USA v. Walli et al.*, Trial Day 2 of 3, May 7, 2013, 279.

25. *U.S. v. Platte*, case nos. 03-1345, 03-1347, 03-1353, decided March 17, 2005, https://caselaw.findlaw.com/us-10th-circuit/1154851.html.

26. Jim Forest, *At Play in the Lions' Den: A Biography and Memoir of Daniel Berrigan* (Maryknoll, NY: Orbis, 2017), 342.

27. *USA v. Walli et al.*, Trial Day 2 of 3, May 7, 2013, 291.

28. *USA v. Walli et al.*, Trial Day 2 of 3, May 7, 2013, 292.

29. *USA v. Walli et al.*, Trial Day 2 of 3, May 7, 2013, 307.

30. *USA v. Walli et al.*, 28 USC Declaration 1749 of Ira C. Helfand, M.D.

31. *USA v. Walli et al.*, 28 USC Section 1749, Declaration of Retired U.S. Catholic Bishop Thomas Gumbleton.

32. Ann Wright, interview with the author, April 25, 2021.

33. *USA v. Walli et al.*, Trial Day 3 of 3, May 8, 2017, 88.

34. *USA v. Walli et al.*, Trial Day 3 of 3, May 8, 2017, 95.

35. *USA v. Walli et al.*, Trial Day 3 of 3, May 8, 2017, 82.

36. *USA v. Walli et al.*, Trial Day 3 of 3, May 8, 2017, 114.

37. *USA v. Walli et al.*, Trial Day 3 of 3, May 8, 2017, 119.

38. *USA v. Walli et al.*, Trial Day 3 of 3, May 8, 2017, 120.

39. *USA v. Walli et al.*, Trial Day 3 of 3, May 8, 2017, 121.

40. *USA v. Walli et al.*, Trial Day 3 of 3, May 8, 2017, 125.

41. *USA v. Walli et al.*, Trial Day 3 of 3, May 8, 2017, 80.

42. Carolyn E. Fulco, Catharyn T. Liverman, and Harold C. Sox, eds., *Gulf War and Health: Volume 1: Depleted Uranium, Sarin,*

Pyridostigmine Bromide, Vaccines (Washington, DC: National Academies Press, 2000), https://www.ncbi.nlm.nih.gov/books/NBK222859; Harald Franzen, "The Science of the Silver Bullet," *Scientific American*, March 5, 2001, https://www.scientificamerican.com/article/the -science-of-the-silver/.

43. *USA v. Walli et al.*, Trial Day 3 of 3, May 8, 2017, 144.
44. *USA v. Walli et al.*, Trial Day 3 of 3, May 8, 2017, 147.
45. *USA v. Walli et al.*, Trial Day 3 of 3, May 8, 2017, 149.
46. *USA v. Walli et al.*, Trial Day 3 of 3, May 8, 2017, 150.
47. *USA v. Walli et al.*, Trial Day 3 of 3, May 8, 2017, 152.
48. *USA v. Walli et al.*, Trial Day 3 of 3, May 8, 2017, 157.
49. *USA v. Walli et al.*, Trial Day 3 of 3, May 8, 2017, 160–61.
50. *USA v. Walli et al.*, Trial Day 3 of 3, May 8, 2017, 161–62.
51. *USA v. Walli et al.*, Trial Day 3 of 3, May 8, 2017, 163.
52. *USA v. Walli et al.*, Trial Day 3 of 3, May 8, 2017, 164–65.
53. *USA v. Walli et al.*, Trial Day 3 of 3, May 8, 2017, 173.
54. *USA v. Walli et al.*, Trial Day 3 of 3, May 8, 2017, 180.
55. *USA v. Walli et al.*, Trial Day 3 of 3, May 8, 2017, 183.
56. *USA v. Walli et al.*, Trial Day 3 of 3, May 8, 2017, 186–87.
57. *USA v. Walli et al.*, Trial Day 3 of 3, May 8, 2017, 194.

Chapter Ten—pages 151–60

1. Paul Magno, email to the author, October 22, 2020.
2. Turin Film Corp., "Ash Wednesday, Festival of Hope, Day 10, Part 11," https://youtu.be/fJbpQTYQzZ4; and "Ash Wednesday, Festival of Hope, Day 10, Part 12," https://youtu.be/kqkOFHqPVlo. Please note that the dates mentioned in the video explanatory predate this Festival of Hope, which took place on March 4, 1981.
3. Proposition One Campaign, "Charlie King Sings to Transform Now! Plowshares, Knoxville TN, 5/6/13," https://youtu.be /Zu2rbbMq0ME. Lyrics reprinted by permission of Charlie King.
4. Friends of Jonah, "James (final)," December 7, 2010, https:// youtu.be/UEox3kFHYnE. Lyrics reprinted with the permission of James Morgan.
5. "Plowshares Supporters at Sentencing Hearing," *Knoxville News-Sentinel*, January 28, 2014, https://youtu.be/NXJYxZLElSk.

6. Art Laffin, "Report on the Transform Now Plowshares Sentencing," *The Nuclear Resister*, February 18, 2014, http://www.nukeresister.org/2014/02/18/prison-sentences-for-three-u-s-nuclear-disarmament-activists/#more-4654.

7. Daniel Berrigan, "Hymn to the New Humanity: Nicaragua, El Salvador, and the U.S., June, 1984," *And the Risen Bread* (New York: Fordham University Press, 1988), 261. Used with permission of Fr. John Dear, literary executor for Daniel Berrigan.

8. Sacred Creation ©1990, Rufino Zaragoza, OFM. Published by OCP. All rights reserved. Used with permission.

9. Quoted in "Absolutely No Remorse," Transform Now Plowshares blog, May 10, 2013, https://transformnowplowshares.wordpress.com/2013/05/10/absolutely-no-remorse/.

10. Constitution *of the United States of America*, Article VI.

11. Anabel Dwyer, interview with the author, April 30, 2021.

12. John Amidon, email to the author, May 9, 2021.

13. Art Laffin, "Eight Arrests at Pentagon Mark Massacre of the Holy Innocents," *The Nuclear Resister*, January 7, 2020.

14. "Six Peace Activists Arrested Blocking Creech Drone Base's Front Gate," *The Nuclear Resister*, April 3, 2019.

15. Jack and Felice Cohen-Joppa, "Please Donate to Help the Nuclear Resister Continue Its Work in 2021!," *The Nuclear Resister*, December 2020.

16. Rosemary Russell, "A Candle: A Call for Peace Placed in the Kitsap Sun," *Ground Zero* 26, no. 1 (January 2021).

Chapter Eleven—pages 161–82

1. Rosalie Riegle, *Doing Time for Peace: Resistance, Family, and Community* (Nashville: Vanderbilt University Press, 2012), 93.

2. Bill Frankel-Streit, interview with the author, July 8, 2020.

3. Turin Film Corp, "Phillip Berrigan, Festival of Hope, Day 9, Part A," https://youtu.be/ZbqXoIbYC1M.

4. John LeMoyne, personal correspondence, Papers of Megan Rice, SHCJ.

5. Megan Rice, "Sentencing Statement of Sr. Megan Rice," *The Nuclear Resister*, February 21, 2014, https://www.nukeresister.org/2014/02/21/sentencing-statement-of-sr-megan-rice/.

6. Susan Crane, "A Reflection on Coming Out of Prison: On Contradictions and Responsibility," *The Nuclear Resister*, May 30, 2012, https://disarmnowplowshares.wordpress.com/2012/05/30/contradictions/.

7. Martha Hennessy, "Prison Reflection," *The Nuclear Resister*, February 11, 2021, https://www.nukeresister.org/2021/02/17/from-fci-danbury-by-nuclear-resister-martha-hennessy-february-11/.

8. Michael Edwards, "To Remain in Prison for the Rest of My Life Is the Greatest Honor You Could Give Me: The Story of Sister Megan Rice," *openDemocracy*, August 18, 2014, https://www.opendemocracy.net/en/transformation/to-remain-in-prison-for-rest-of-my-life-is-greatest-honor-you-could-g/.

9. Linda Stasi, "EXCLUSIVE: 84-year-old Activist Nun Imprisoned in Brooklyn Jail Hellhole for Breaking into Nuclear Facility, Exposing Security Flaws," *New York Daily News*, January 19, 2015, https://www.nydailynews.com/new-york/brooklyn/exclusive-nun-84-brooklyn-jail-hellhole-activism-article-1.2083481.

10. Ellen Barfield, interview with author, January 4, 2021.

11. John Amidon, email to the author, May 23, 2021.

12. Rosalie G. Riegle, *Crossing the Line: Nonviolent Resisters Speak Out for Peace* (Eugene, OR: Wipf and Stock, 2013), 317.

13. Crane, "A Reflection on Coming Out of Prison."

14. Crane, "A Reflection on Coming Out of Prison."

15. Crane, "A Reflection on Coming Out of Prison."

16. Riegle, *Crossing the Line*, 317.

17. Gregory Boertje-Obed and Michele Naar-Obed, "From USP Leavenworth . . . with a Reflection from His Wife, Michele Naar-Obed," *The Nuclear Resister,* July 27, 2014, https://www.nukeresister.org/2014/07/27/from-usp-leavenworth-by-greg-boertje-obed-with-a-reflection-from-his-wife-michele-naar-obed/.

18. Michael Gallagher, *Laws of Heaven: Catholic Activists Today* (New York: Houghton Mifflin Harcourt, 1992), 124.

19. Paul Magno, interview with the author, September 7, 2018.

20. Proposition One Campaign, "Charlie King Sings to Transform Now! Plowshares, Knoxville TN, 5/6/13," https://youtu.be/Zu2rbbMq0ME.

21. Sue Frankel-Streit, interview with the author, July 8, 2020.

22. Jackie Allen-Douçot, interview with the author, July 8, 2020.

23. Martin Newell, interview with the author, June 3, 2020.

24. Clare Grady, interview with the author, May 26, 2020.

25. Frank Cordaro, interview with the author, June 15, 2020.

26. Molly Rush, email to the author, July 13, 2020.

27. Michael Walli, "Elevating the Host," *The Nuclear Resister*, August 16, 2013, https://www.nukeresister.org/2013/08/16/from-the-irwin-county-detention-center-by-michael-walli-2/.

28. Boertje-Obed and Naar-Obed, "From USP Leavenworth."

29. Megan Rice, SHCJ, "From MDC Brooklyn by Sr. Megan Rice, Imprisoned Nuclear Disarmament Activist," *The Nuclear Resister*, December 10, 2014, https://www.nukeresister.org/2015/01/05/from-mdc-brooklyn-by-sr-megan-rice-imprisoned-nuclear-disarmament-activist/.

30. Boertje-Obed and Naar-Obed, "From USP Leavenworth."

31. Berrigan and Wilcox, *Fighting the Lamb's War: Skirmishes with the American Empire* (Monroe, ME: Common Courage Press 1996), 90.

32. Rice, "From MDC Brooklyn."

33. LocalRadioFrance, "Megan Rice—Washington Post Interview 2013," https://youtu.be/S1KvFQ-4oVY.

34. Riegle, *Crossing the Line*, 319.

35. Martha Hennessy, "Changing the Social Order," Kings Bay Plowshares 7 website, May 9, 2021, https://kingsbayplowshares7.org/2021/05/martha-hennessy-changing-the-social-order-may-9-2021/.

36. Rice, "From MDC Brooklyn."

37. Steve Kelly, SJ, interview with the author, December 13, 2017.

38. See Albert Woodfox with Leslie George, *Solitary: Unbroken by Four Decades in Solitary Confinement: My Story of Transformation and Hope* (New York: Grove Press, 2019).

39. Michael Walli, "From FCI McKean," *The Nuclear Resister*, June 5, 2015, http://www.nukeresister.org/2015/05/25/from-fci-mckean-by-michael-walli-shortly-before-his-sudden-release-from-prison/.

40. Boertje-Obed and Naar-Obed, "From USP Leavenworth."

41. Boertje-Obed and Naar-Obed, "From USP Leavenworth."

42. Rice, interview with the author, February 8, 2018.

43. Rice, interview with the author, February 8, 2018.

44. United States Holocaust Memorial Museum, "The White Rose Opposition Movement," *Holocaust Encyclopedia*, https://encyclopedia .ushmm.org/content/en/article/white-rose. See also further information from the White Rose Foundation website, https://www.weisse-rose -stiftung.de.

45. Arthur J. Laffin, *Swords into Plowshares: A Chronology of Plowshares Disarmament Actions, 1980–2003*, foreword by Daniel Berrigan (Marion, SD: Rose Hill Books, 2003), 33–34.

46. Judith Martin, "Protest Dress," *Miss Manners' Guide for the Turn-of-the-Millennium* (New York: Touchstone, 1990), 138.

Chapter Twelve—pages 183–92

1. United States Court of Appeals, Sixth Circuit, *United States of America v. Michael R. Walli; Megan Rice; Greg Boertje-Obed*, Nos. 14–5220, 14–5221, 14–5222, https://caselaw.findlaw.com/us-6th -circuit/1700452.html.

2. United States Court of Appeals, Sixth Circuit, *United States of America v. Michael R. Walli; Megan Rice; Greg Boertje-Obed*, Nos. 14–5220, 14–5221, 14–5222.

3. Ralph Hutchison, press release, "Court Suggests Decision May Lead to Release of Rice, Boertje-Obed and Walli," *The Nuclear Resister*, May 8, 2015, https://www.nukeresister.org/2015/05/08/sabotage -conviction-overturned-new-sentence-ordered-for-transform-now -plowshares/.

4. Ardeth Platte, email to the author, September 26, 2020.

5. John LaForge, "Nuclear Weapons Protesters' Sabotage Convic- tion Overturned," *The Nuclear Resister*, May 12, 2015, https://www .nukeresister.org/2015/05/08/sabotage-conviction-overturned-new -sentence-ordered-for-transform-now-plowshares/.

6. Edith Roberts, "Potential Nominee Profile: Amul Thapar," SCO- TUSblog, July 3, 2018, https://www.scotusblog.com/2018/07/potential -nominee-profile-amul-thapar.

7. Roberts, "Potential Nominee Profile: Amul Thapar."

8. Megan Hooke Tourlis and Tim Pettolina, interview with the author, January 29, 2021.

9. Gregory Boertje-Obed, interview with the author, May 20, 2018.

10. Gregory Boertje-Obed, interview with the author, May 20, 2018.

11. FriendsofJonah, "Steve Kelly SJ speaks about Plowshares Actions," November 8, 2010, https://youtu.be/LASoPrTqTtI.

12. "Open Letter from the Brooklyn Metropolitan Detention Center from Sr. Megan Rice, on Behalf of the Transform Now Plowshares," Transform Now Plowshares blog, July 28, 2014, https://transformnowplowshares.wordpress.com/2014/07/28/second-anniversary-statement-from-megan-michael-greg/.

Index